MJ $
Thanks

SHIELDED

SUFFERING

Enjoy

MJ & Bri,
Thanks for your support!

SHIELDED

SUFFERING

THE ESCAPE ARTIST
A.J. Nystrom

CRUSH COMPLACENCY LIFE & CAREER COACHING

Raynham Center, MA 2016

To contact the author, please visit the following:

www.youtube.com/crushcomplacency
www.CrushComplacency.com
www.facebook.com/crushcomplacency
www.twitter.com/c_complacency
www.instagram.com/crushcomplacency

For information regarding special discounts for bulk purchases
please contact A.J. at AJ@CrushComplacency.com

Printed in the United States of America
First Printing, 2016

ISBN 978-0-692-74616-5

Crush Complacency Life & Career Coaching,
PO Box 622, Raynham Center, MA 02678
www.CrushComplacency.com

DEDICATION

This is for all the people- fellow students, fellow correction officers and federal agents, fellow first responders and public servants, and anyone else that has ever felt that they couldn't live another day, fought valiantly and succumbed to their demons.

For all those who have spoken up and inspired me to share my story. For those that read this story and are inspired to speak up. Thank you for your bravery, courage, strength, vulnerability, and accessibility. Let our voices and pens unite to lead the world to a brighter, healthier, more inclusive tomorrow.

ACKNOWLEDGMENTS

Thanks to Amy Poole of Be Focused Photography in Taunton, Massachusetts. Her patience and expertise was greatly appreciated during my first photo shoot as a professional. She was ready, willing, and able to work with my crazy schedule and got me to come out of my shell for some great shots- a few of which are found on the cover and back pages of this book. Check her out at Facebook.com/BeFocusedMA

Thanks to Melissa Kinney of Purple Spider Graphics in Berkley, Massachusetts. I have been working with Melissa for over five years and she has assisted me in bringing my designs and ideas to life... That's not entirely true. She's responsible for taking my pedestrian, haphazard sketches and transforming them into superlative works of art. I was elated when she agreed to assist me on this cover design. I highly recommend her for anyone looking to distance themselves from their competition, or just looking to turn their doodles and concepts into the "real deal." Check out her amazing and extensive work at Facebook.com/PurpleSpiderGraphics.

Thank you to my friends, colleagues, and clients that so graciously dedicated their time and attention to reading through drafts of this book. I'm grateful for your honest reflections and heartfelt suggestions about my story. I thank you for lending your eyes to catch my mistakes and your hearts to remind me of stories or tidbits of information you felt would be compelling additions. Without your words of encouragement and implorations, this book would not be published and would've remained just a really thick pamphlet I gave my clients to peruse.

CONTENTS

PART I:
BEFORE WE BEGIN

Preface

Flashback to December, 2014. Specifically, December 25th, 2014: Christmas Day. I'm lucky enough to be spending Christmas with my family and *not* getting ready for work- by the way, I'm a correction officer at one of the two maximum security facilities in Massachusetts. As the day drew to a close I remembered that it's Thursday and I had Christmas Day off last year, as well. Out of curiosity, I charted out the major holidays for the next few years and looked at my fate. Not a single major holiday off (aside from Thanksgiving which always falls on a Thursday) until Independence Day, July 4th, 2018!

I started the grieving process- more accurately, I started the seething process. I had to make a change. I had already started making significant changes in my life but I needed to commit to major changes that would allow me to live the life that I wanted and, quite honestly, needed. I wanted to help people improve their quality of life and strengthen the fabric of my community while being well compensated and being able to take time off to enjoy life and recharge my batteries whenever necessary.

Hey, you can't save the world if you can't save yourself, first! A few things needed to happen before my goals could be achieved, or become even remotely feasible:

1. Get myself right. Seek mental health care.
   We'll take about that in the coming pages.
2. Become certified as a life coach
   Mission: Accomplished in March, 2016!
   (Associate Certified Coach through the
   International Coach Federation)
3. Tell my story…

I'd like to take this opportunity to warmly welcome you to Step #3. I hope your stay is enjoyable, entertaining, educational, and emotional. The writing process sure was.

A.J. Nystrom
"The Escape Artist"
June 22nd, 2016

Warning

I'm quite sure that there aren't many books that have begun with a warning (the only ones I have seen are The Structure of Magic Part I and II by Dr. Richard Bandler and Dr. John Grinder) but I believe it's wholeheartedly appropriate in this case. As someone diagnosed and challenged by Post Traumatic Stress Disorder, I have been triggered to recall haunting, abusive, and difficult instances of my past by people speaking about situations in a nonchalant, fairly unaffected manner. They didn't know any better because- up to this point, if they read this book- they don't know I have PTSD and they didn't know they were triggering me. It's not their fault, it's not my fault, it's truly not anyone's fault. It's something I willfully chose to endure at that point in my life. I have since learned tactics and mechanisms to employ in order to minimize the likelihood of being triggered and lessen the effects when I am triggered. I am much more loving and accepting of myself than I've ever been and I allow myself to be excused from a discussion if it is too difficult for me to negotiate. I wish to give fair notice to anyone and everyone that this may be a difficult book to read. It is very detailed and, at times, very graphic. I felt it was necessary to leave no stone unturned and to write the 100% unbridled, uncensored, no holds barred truth. It's the only way that I can say I held nothing back. Not holding back or censoring myself is a commitment I have made and it's a promise to myself that I intend to keep.

I'd like to call your attention to how I identified my PTSD. I said it's something I'm challenged by. As you will learn, I'm a bit of a word nerd and I feel that the words we use influence our approach to things in life. So, in this case, saying that I "suffer" from PTSD may suggest or indicate that I have resigned myself to the control of the disorder, I have lost, there's no going back, and there's nothing I can do about it. That's not how I operate. By saying that I am "challenged" by PTSD, it brings the disorder down a few notches to a more pedestrian, manageable level. I'm challenged to eat healthy and to work out. I am challenged to grow my business, Crush Complacency, and to provide for myself and my family. I'm challenged to improve as a certified life coach and career developer so I can achieve my goals of improving the quality of life for my clients and assisting them obtain their desired results. In that mindset, PTSD is another challenge within my day rather than an insurmountable peak in the distance. I'll get into this concept more later in the book, but I wanted to bring it to your attention now so you'll be more mindful of the language throughout this book, in that sense.

What we are about to embark on is the hardest thing I've ever done. We have heard throughout our lives of people having skeletons in their closet. I wholeheartedly subscribe to this idea. I believe that the skeletons are instances and memories from our past that we have allowed to lie around decomposing and getting in the way of our pursuit of our true greatness. I believe everyone has them and few people ever acknowledge them. I have been fortunate enough, and I've worked hard enough, that I have not only acknowledged them but I've become *comfortable* enough in my *discomfort* to be able to call them individually by name when I enter the closet. Also, like a spring cleaning, I have organized and stacked my skeletons in the back of my closet so I can still use the closet to store more positive, useful things in my life. I think this metaphor is important because there is no illusion that my skeletons have disappeared. They are certainly still there but I have learned to work with them and around them. I have also grown to the point of self awareness and self acceptance that I fully disclose everything to people in my life, as well. Initially, being that blunt, open, and honest about something that is seen as a sociocultural stigma such as mental health challenges, it knocks people for a loop and their initial reaction is to create distance. However, as they gradually realize "mental health challenges" is not the same as "clinically insane" they begin to slowly appreciate the upfront honesty and "realness."

We're going to travel into my closet together in order to identify and examine some of the skeletons that call my closet their home. The purpose of this is to reveal the sad state of affairs and some dark areas of our culture in order to promote positive self exploration and self care for everyone, and to help us help other people along the way. I've carried this dead weight, this darkness into and out of relationships, through state and federal law enforcement academies, and through many good and bad times. Over time, it truly grew to be a part of me. Hell, for the longest time I thought I was fine. "The past is in the past and I've moved on." In reality, I wasn't normal. We'll dive more into this topic later on, as well.

You will not see any names in here. No one will be identified by their legal name. I do not mention the place I grew up or where I went to school, the school's name, any teachers, students, or even my parents. The names are not important because this story could take place anywhere and happen to anyone. This book isn't about vengeance or revenge. This isn't about people losing their jobs or having their lives destroyed. This book is about helping others directly and indirectly to come to grips with the realities of bullying, mental health challenges, loneliness and hurt. This is intended to help start the conversation about trauma and suicide in our law enforcement and public service communities. This is about freeing ourselves from the darkness of our past or even our present and live life in a new light. This is to remove the stigma, break down the wall, pull back the curtain, and rip down the veil that hides mental health challenges. If we are totally honest with ourselves, I firmly believe that everyone can benefit from regular visits with a mental health professional.

There will be some strong language in this book. There is going to be some graphic, derogatory, vulgar, salty language in the following pages. They will be words that my classmates and coworkers have said to me. In other words the use of strong, adult language will be to illustrate direct quotes, not vulgarity on my part. These pages are filled with the darkest times of my life and the hand written manuscript was soaked with tears on more than a few occasions. This is the literary equivalent of opening my chest and baring myself in the deepest, most intimate, most vulnerable way possible so that others may learn, benefit, grieve for me, with me, and for themselves, and so I may teach and lead others.

Someone had to start the conversation. Only a few have spoken up thus far so I feel obligated to add my voice and my story to the crowd. The experiences I have had, the talents that I have honed, and the positions that I have held have come together to create a sense of duty to speak about my experiences by utilizing my talents. I got into law enforcement to help people, to improve their quality of life, and to strengthen the fabric of our society. In uniform I was unable to help as many people as I wanted- and those few I *was* able to help, I wasn't able to help as much as I wanted, either. Now that I am out of uniform, I hope that I'll be able to help as many people as possible as much as possible, especially those that are still in uniform that need a voice or a helping hand.

Another aspect of the language in this book (I warned you, I am a word nerd) that I haven't seen employed much, if at all in other books, is how you, the reader, is addressed. I have read many self-help, psychology, videography, finance, public speaking, business, and coaching books and one trend I'm not thrilled about is that the reader is written to in a harsh, direct tone- usually utilizing the pronoun "you." I don't care to be talked down to, I don't believe anybody cares to be talked down to, and I don't wish to come off as talking down to my audience. I'm no better than anyone else and, since you're reading this, we have some common ground and you should be addressed in an inclusive manner and on a level playing field. Honestly, I use "we" and "us" in all of my writing because I count myself as part of the audience. This book is as much for me as it is for everyone else. I'm always learning and continuously gaining insight on a lot of this material. We're all in this together so we should speak and write like it.

Introduction

I have had a plan to kill myself since I was twelve years old. Let's face facts, there's no easy way to broach the topic of suicide, bullying, Post Traumatic Stress Disorder, Depression, or Anxiety so we might as well get it out of the way up front. If you were to ask any of my friends, family, colleagues, teachers, bosses, or hell, anyone that came in contact with me over the course of this half of my lifetime they would most likely describe me as a well put together, intelligent, respectful, eloquent, thoughtful young man with wonderful speaking abilities, leadership qualities, and the knack for talking to anyone between the ages of 5 and 95 and being able to find common ground to share a conversation with them. Perfect. My plan worked well and my act fooled them. I am not a mental health professional. I am a patient.

There is no easy way for me to talk about being bullied, being depressed, and wanting to kill myself. However, it's a discussion we need to have. For over half my life I carried an idea with me that I could end my life whenever I wanted. I had a place, I had a time of day, I had a method, and I had plenty of reasons... I had everything in place. I believe the reason I'm alive and here today is to illustrate that the good outweighs the bad, to share how my plan to kill myself has been transformed into a plan to help others, and to pull back the curtain on a few big topics: bullying and therapy.

I'm certain that this book will hurt people- family, friends, former teachers and classmates, people in my church community, coworkers, and maybe even people I've never met before. Please realize that this isn't about you. It's not even about me. This is about assisting the people in our present world to get the treatment that they need. It is tough to take that initial step when we have been brought to the point of trusting no one only to find we must reach out of our Comfort Zone to find a helping hand. My hope is that this book, beyond the horrors of my story, is the helping hand that can meet someone *in* their Comfort Zone and begin that conversation with them on their own terms. I hope that the people in my life do not hold themselves accountable and beat themselves up over signs that they missed. There weren't many signs to pick up. This was done intentionally. I hid what was happening to me because I was embarrassed and ashamed- and I was really good at hiding it, too. Do not hold yourself accountable for what happened, but make a commitment to improve yourself going forward. Turn this into a positive. That's my goal with this book and my goal for everyone who reads this book- turn it into a positive.

This is also for all of us, those of us that need help and the people who want to help or at least become more educated in helping others. There is so much fluff talk out there about taking action and helping others that lacks substance. Sure, they're pretty words and they inspire people to do *something*, but they fail to instruct people on *what to do*. Not many people have been providing solid, concrete ways to help- this book is different. I will go through the signs I hid, how I hid them, and how they can be discovered- perhaps the most important things we will need is an empathetic heart, patience, and a willingness to have a conversation. I could apologize but that solves nothing. The truth is that I didn't want anyone to know. Honestly, I don't know if I'm ready for people to know now, but that's part of becoming comfortable in my discomfort. Hold your nose, take a big breath, and join me for a jump in the deep end. Frank Oz, the inimitable Muppeteer who voiced and gave life to Miss Piggy said about puppeteering, "In order for it to look good up there [in front of the cameras- AJN] I have to be uncomfortable down here." Although I'm not operating a puppet to entertain anyone, in much the same fashion the best way to reach people in their Comfort Zone is to leave my own Comfort Zone. Fasten your seatbelts and please keep all hands, feet, and other extremities in the vehicle until the ride comes to a complete stop.

SHIELDED

SUFFERING

PART II: MIDDLE SCHOOL/ HIGH SCHOOL

6th Grade

It's September 1995. I am an 11-year-old entering my 6th grade year at the local private middle school. This is a great opportunity to get a new start. I made it a focal point to identify, introduce myself to, and connect with kids that I considered to be cool. Cool kids were defined by cool jackets and cool haircuts. A cool jacket was usually the Starter brand jackets with the large logo of your favorite team on the back. The cool hairstyle of the day was to grow your hair out on top and part it down the middle into either a "bowl" cut or brush to the side and let the hair curl in front of your face. I got the cheaper, newer Starter jacket with the small logo on the front and I had a short, spiked haircut. I instantly started at a disadvantage due to the pop culture-based hierarchy of middle school.

I was a kid of average height, average weight, average looks, above average intelligence, and had teeth that would need the attention of an orthodontist in the next few years. My claims to fame were my pitching prowess on the local Little League Baseball fields and I had been taking drum lessons for about 2 ½ years. My Little League team had just won the League Championship but we lost in the City Championship. I was known as one of the top pitchers in the city. On the drumming front, I was about to get my first drumset and I was saving diligently to buy it. I was working two paper routes that totaled over 120 houses in the area. I would put most of the money into long term savings (because my parents told me that I had to) and put the rest away for my drumset. I knew my ticket to being established and respected as a "cool kid" was going to come on the baseball field and behind the drumset.

As the law of averages would have it, I was *too* average. I don't know why I was marginalized. Perhaps I marginalized myself. I was what I would describe as a boy apart (my apologies to Vin Diesel and his 2003 film, *A Man Apart*). Essentially, I was too smart to hang out with the dumb kids (I say that relatively speaking: we didn't have anybody that had any developmental challenges or severe learning disabilities) but not smart enough to hang out with the smart kids and be considered a nerd. I was too athletic to hang out with the "walkers," (the kids that walked around the court or field to fulfill their participation requirement for gym class) but I was not athletic enough to be called a jock. I was too cool (by my own assessment) to hang out with the outcasts but I wasn't cool enough to be a cool kid. It seemed that I was just different enough not to fit in anywhere. (God bless Steve Jobs and his penchant for "round pegs in square holes," etc.)

The bullying started innocuously enough. We called it razzing or kidding. We made fun of people's hair. Kids that had to get glasses were razzed about it. Weight was another favorite target. The key to a good razzing or kidding was to not take things too personally or seriously. Needless to say, as an empathetic, hormone filled pre-teen I took everything personally and seriously. I *sucked* at being razzed. The kids would pick on me unyieldingly and I defended everything about myself that they took aim at. My hair was weird because I was growing it out (although every attempt was thwarted by my mom's insistence on getting a haircut). I wasn't fat or heavy, my clothes just didn't fit right. Whatever joke, slight, or slam they threw I absorbed like an uppercut from Mike Tyson and responded with a feeble jab of my own to counterattack.

They enjoyed this. They saw their shots were connecting and they knew I could feel it – so they kept going. "Your mom" this and "your dad" that added up. They made it very personal and tailored their jokes, jabs, and verbal beat downs specifically to my weaknesses and what I cared about most.

Why do we defend ourselves against the opinions of others? Reflecting on my own situation, I think it was equal parts pride and acknowledgment. The component of pride comes in due to our desire to fit in and to be a respected member of the group. There's strength, safety, structure, nourishment, and acceptance in the group. It was a simple equation: if you're not with us, you're against us. It was always better to be with the group. It was always better to be with *a* group. If someone is excommunicated from a society they face almost certain death. They have no protection against wildlife and thieves, nowhere permanent to sleep or get food, and they have no one to work with in order to accomplish something bigger than themselves. The other component is acknowledgement. Reflect a little with me, if you will. If someone comes at us with something that is way off base and has no basis in truth or fact, then we most likely will have no issue ignoring the vitriol. However, if there is even a little bit of truth- or at least similar opinion- we set out to deny, defend, and deflect. I would tell them I wasn't fat, then create an excuse or explanation for my parents, then I inevitably found a similar characteristic of someone else that they could hopefully leave me to make fun of.

The Cool Kids

In my efforts to fit in and gain respect among my peers I
needed to find favor with a leader. I identified a boy in my
grade that hung out with a group of boys that, based purely on
looks, appeared to be a group of cool kids. It was evident that
he was the leader. When he got up, everyone got up. Where he
went, everyone followed. If I got in with him I would make
quick friends and be all set. They had the cool jackets and they
had the cool haircuts so they *had* to be cool by my
calculations. Most of them were musicians (or at least aspiring
musicians) but they had no drummer- I had an instant "in."
They liked some of the bands that I liked and the bands I
didn't know I instantly became a fan, strictly by proxy.

Leader, as I'll call him, made the call. If he liked you, you
were all set. If he didn't like you, you were the new target.
Where Leader led, the followers followed. It was an easy
equation to solve. My introduction to Leader was a game of
Red Dot hacky sack. If you let the hacky sack drop, you
received a red dot- a welt or bruise courtesy of someone
throwing the hacky sack at you as hard as they could. I soon
realized that Leader did not like me when I was being set up
and targeted for several "red dots" in a row.

Leader was known as a bad boy. He routinely acted up in
class, got poor grades, and was the most likely aggressor in

any fight at the school. It was Leader's volatility that kept him at the helm- none of the followers really wanted to get on his bad side. Although Leader wasn't necessarily the biggest or strongest kid around, what he lacked he made up for in tenacity.

I recall pulling up to the school one morning to see a group huddle towards the far side of the driveway- a fight. Leader was wailing away at a younger boy who was obviously overmatched. Leader landed a flurry of punches triggering a medical condition in his adversary that resulted in a seizure. Leader kept going. As the younger boy collapsed to the ground, Leader rained down left after right after left after right. He did. Not. Care. Eventually, my mom and a local lawyer whose kids went to the school pulled Leader off of his vanquished opponent (victim?) and attended to the poor pummeled kid. This set the tone for Leader. That was a power-play move and an assurance that everyone knew he was incapable of caring about anyone that should cross him.

7ᵗʰ Grade

The summer of 1996 was filled with a ton of baseball and I was entirely in my element. It was my final year of eligibility for Little League, I was made a captain on my team, and I was one of the top pitchers in the city. Early in the summer, before the regular season even began, my league team won a tournament. Then our team lost only one game the entire regular season and playoffs to win the League Championship for the second year in a row. Then we went on to win the City Championship in a really close series against two guys that I would play the next six years with in Babe Ruth and Senior Babe Ruth baseball leagues. I was selected to the top All-Star team and we won the District Championship. We went on to the state tournament but I believe we were eliminated in the semifinals. I pitched really well that year and earned a nickname for my curveball that would follow me for as long as I played baseball- Captain Hook. I was getting a lot better with my drumming and I thought I was ready to start or join a band. I had had a successful and enjoyable summer. I was ready for the opportunity to move my way up the social hierarchy armed with my fresh, new athletic achievements.

Around November of my seventh grade year, despite all the verbal hazing, razzing, and abuse I had received so far, I made a push to get in with the cool kids and tried to start a band with the followers who played instruments. This didn't go over well and was the catalyst for what turned out to be the most violent period of my life.

Confidant

During this turbulent time of my life I was fortunate to find an adult figure with an unbiased view point - my maternal grandfather. One important aspect of any personal care regiment is consistency. I had such that consistency with my grandfather during the fall and spring weeks because I spent a considerable amount of time over his house. While my mom worked as a retail pharmacist and dad went off to his bowling league, I went over my maternal grandparents' house and had quality time with my grandfather. We would take rides in his truck or spend time in his office/ study in the basement. I emptied my heart out to him about struggling to make friends, talking to girls, and the bullying. He would listen ever so patiently, clarifying and rewording things as I went along, and then repeated my dilemmas back to me. I would later learn, while training to become a certified life coach, that these are techniques taught to create trust with a person and develop a deeper understanding of where they are coming from. He was my own self-appointed life coach and mentor. Then he shared his experiences of evaluating friends, assessing his self worth, and, in general how to be a proper man. We would have these heart-to-heart talks over ice cream or while buying baseball cards. Perhaps that's why am still wildly addicted to both! Whatever I threw at him he had the right thing to say. Whether he shared his own struggles with a similar situation or told a story about someone else in history overcoming long odds or significant difficulties to achieve their greatness, my grandfather was able to assure me that I was not alone and that I could overcome whatever was thrown my way.

Grandfather's Legacy of Learning

My grandfather was the consummate educator. In order to be a great educator one must be a great student and learner, as well. As a young child, I spent a lot of time at the high school where my grandfather was the superintendent. I always noticed a large rolling library rack in his office but I never gave much thought to it. My grandfather loved books and loved knowledge. He was thirsty for information and never stopped learning. He had a Master's in Education and a Master's in English. He was even pursuing his Doctorate in Education after his retirement. His study, a small room in the basement with a television and a fireplace, had a writing desk and respectable sized bookshelf overflowing with books on leadership, writing, public speaking, public administration, politics, education, special education (some of the titles from the 1950s and 60s I cannot repeat in polite company due to political correctness), psychology, philosophy, and economics. As a child I never paid much attention to the books. After I began this journey, this transition to a life of helping others, I rediscovered his study and I was amazed- and somewhat emboldened- to learn that some of the books that grace his shelves now also grace mine.

I've learned through the years that my grandfather impacted many more lives than just mine. Remember that library rack full of textbooks in his office? Part of being in the administration while he was in the school was attending detention. My grandfather loved working detention. It was his opportunity to go where the help was needed. After all, rarely did good students get in enough trouble to warrant a detention. The textbooks in the library rack were every textbook for every subject in every grade in the school. Detention turned into a tutoring session with my grandfather at the helm. I've heard from several former students that they'd show up to detention without getting in trouble just to receive his help. He felt that punishment was useless if correction and improvement of behavior and performance were not included in the package. Still today, students that are all grown up with children of their own will stop me at a restaurant or on the street to share with me a moment of my grandfather's wisdom, compassion, or firm but fair discipline and I smile knowing that I have willfully and thoughtfully sought to develop the same qualities in the hopes- allow me to correct myself- the *pursuit* of being even half the man he was.

New Weapons

As 7th grade progresses, what started as verbal attacks began
to get physical. Words became punches, punches became
kicks, and in short order they increased their arsenal to include
pieces of their uniform as weapons. The shoes weren't bad
because most of us had small feet and wore boat shoes
because they were comfortable. Those were usually long-
range projectiles that I could dodge or block fairly easily if I
saw the attack coming. I remember one kid had wing tips.
Those hurt badly, especially if I caught a thick wooden heel or
a pointed toe. During the very end of the year it became much
easier to know when someone was going to throw a shoe. The
movie Austin Powers: International Man of Mystery was
released in May 1997. When one of Dr. Evil's henchmen, Odd
Job, throws a shoe that hits Austin Powers in the head, Powers
yells, "Who throws a shoe, honestly?!" One of the followers
couldn't help himself but to snicker that line quietly just as
someone was winding up to throw their shoe at me. I took that
as my cue to either duck, move out of the way, or- if I was
feeling particularly reflexive- turn around to attempt to catch
the shoe and to return fire. They also started to use a kinder,
gentler version of a softball- don't let that description fool you
because, although it was lacking that hard plastic exterior, it
still had tremendous weight to it and the balls could pack a

nasty wallop. Thankfully, these balls were used very sparingly and often used only as intimidation. The followers would take turns getting a running start and throw the ball as hard as possible against the wall right next to my head as I was changing. Occasionally, they'd throw from a full pitcher's windup (no running start) and hit me square in the middle of the back.

It was during this time that I leaned heavily on my grandfather for support and advice. I was embarrassed, demoralized, and desperate. He regularly encouraged me to start talking to people in position to make decisions and take action. He even went as far as to encourage me to defend myself by any means necessary in order to avoid getting hurt worse. One thing that I requested of him during this whole ordeal was that he not tell my Mom what was going on. I didn't want her to worry about me and I knew she would freak out, overreact, and take action by going to the school to speak directly with the Principal, during school hours, with me in tow, directly in front of the kids that were the cause of it all.

Coach

I don't recall the first time I spoke to someone about being bullied and harassed but I do remember I spoke with the gym teacher. The gym teacher (baseball coach, basketball coach, etc.-it was a small school and the coaching was pretty much a one man show) is someone I'll simply refer to as Coach. Coach was everyone's friend and was eager to get along with everyone. Anything he could let kids get away with without disciplining them, he did. He only took disciplinary action when he was instructed and supervised to do so. I know I didn't say anything until seventh grade after things started to get physical because there was no bodily harm until then and we were conditioned that verbal harassment was part of growing up. I do know that when I told Coach about the boys being assaultive for the first time I found him in his office, the equipment closet in the boys' locker room, after school. The equipment locker was a fenced in area with a padlock on it that housed all the school's gym and sports equipment… and a small desk and bookshelf for Coach to keep his paperwork. When I initially told him he brushed things off saying that he didn't have time for that kind of stuff and suggested that I talk to the kids. After that technique didn't work I returned to him, hoping that he would take me seriously and offer some assistance. This time he asked who the kids were by name and

I named them. He chuckled and told me to man up and defend myself because I'm the same size as a few of them and bigger than the others. I told him that the size advantage was erased when more than one person attacked me at the same time and that was always the case... no exceptions. He told me that it was a part of growing up, I'd have to suck it up and handle it. Part of his reasoning why he couldn't and wouldn't discipline them or even talk to them about it was because he hadn't witnessed anything and it would be my word against theirs, even though I showed him bruises and other injuries caused by them.

Coach had a point. In order for a case to be presented in court we need evidence of the crime. I had no fresh evidence. Of course I felt unheard, ignored, and made out to be less than human but I now knew what I needed in order for Coach to listen to me. If he bumped up every complaint or investigated every accusation made in that middle school, he would need a second person to run class. However, due to how severe my claims were and the presence of older evidence, I figured he would have taken my words a bit more seriously. However, and this isn't the last time I'll bring this up, bullying wasn't the well-publicized, well known problem that it is now. Claims of bullying were treated as "kids being kids," and "part of growing up." Even fights were treated much less severely than they are now. Teachers would check to make sure both kids were OK, send them to the nurse (separately) to get cleaned up, and the combatants were given detention. In order for my accusations to be taken seriously, Coach would have to witness the abuse first hand or see fresh evidence of abuse. On several occasions Coach was not in his office when the bullying and harassment took place (actually, for 90+% of the abuse he was not present). He was upstairs usually leaning or sitting on the stage at the front of the gymnasium. That was understandable because he had to proctor the changing of classes and make sure both boys and girls got changed and off to class in an expedient fashion.

"Look for the Helpers"

As seventh-grade began to develop into hell on earth, a strange thing happened. People started to notice changes in my body language, temperament, and performance. Two teachers in particular were instrumental in assisting me through this difficult period. They turned into the people I could approach with issues and concerns. They were the sounding boards that fielded the fears, worries, anxieties, depression, and apprehension. Unfortunately, although those two teachers were willing to listen, offer advice, and help me where they could, they were unable to do anything to physically stop the attacks from happening. I didn't feel comfortable approaching the male teachers and the female teachers weren't allowed in the locker room. I was between a rock and a hard place trying to get help.

Fred Rogers, a.k.a. Mr. Rogers from the PBS show *Mr. Rogers' Neighborhood*, is credited with saying, "When I was a boy I would see scary things in the news. My mother would say to me, 'Look for the helpers. You will always find people who are helping.'" This was certainly the case in my situation. However, I had such a difficult time even finding myself that it was nearly impossible to see the immense impact those two teachers had on my life in that moment.

To anyone struggling, adult or child, look for the helpers. This is solid advice from someone that has been there and, in all honesty, is still there from time to time. There is someone in your life that is there to help you. You are *never* alone. The hardest part, sometimes, is having the strength and the guts to look up and to look around for the outstretched hand. We may feel that the world is out to get us and beat us down. I get it. I've been there. Sometimes I slip back there, as well. Have the courage to look up and look around. In the midst of all the fists coming down, all the haters, the judgments, the biases, and opinions there will be at least one hand outstretched looking to pull you up and lead you to safety. If you are finding it difficult to see a helper and you don't see any hands outstretched then please look at this book. I have placed my personal email address and phone number in here numerous times. I am a helper. I got into law enforcement to help others and I have been fortunate to mold my career around the desire to help as many people as possible, as much as possible. I am the only person to read my emails and I will respond as quickly as possible. I can be reached at AJ@CrushComplacency.com.

Principal/ Guidance Counselor

My seventh grade homeroom teacher was the first person to encourage me to speak with the Principal. I would become well acquainted with that office over the next year and a half. The Principal's office was to the left after entering the front door and walking up the stairs. I recall a solid wooden door with some decorative carvings. A dark colored carpet (blue, I believe) greeted me as I opened the door that led to a small entryway before opening up into the full office. The furniture all matched and it was all hardwood with dark stain and sparse vinyl or leather upholstery on the chair arms and back. The desk was an executive style writing desk. The Principal was very stern with a serious demeanor. I don't ever remember feeling welcomed in their presence. Every interaction was terse, calculated, and businesslike. Our initial talk only last a few minutes before I was dismissed with the parting instruction to talk things out with the boys. When I was encouraged to attempt to resolve the situation peacefully, I didn't know what to think. I had tried to handle it peacefully. I spoke with my direct teacher numerous times and they did not do anything to stop or report what was happening. I had spoken to other teachers about what was going on and one of them felt it was appropriate to send me to the Principal's office and their initial response was to try to talk to the boys again. I don't recall if that discussion ever took place. I highly doubt it because I firmly believe I was smart enough to discern what fate would befall me if I attempted to extend an olive branch to Leader and the followers.

When that attempt obviously failed, I returned to their office on my own, since they extended the obligatory, halfhearted "If you need to talk again my door is always open and I'm always available," offer. Frustrated, I informed them that speaking with the boys didn't end favorably. At this point they suggested that I speak with Coach and try to handle things through him. I informed the Principal that I had spoken to Coach numerous times about these incidents, nothing had been done, and none of the students had been spoken to. They instructed me to speak with Coach again at a time when I didn't have any new abuse to report and they would speak with Coach on their own, as well. I cannot confirm if that talk ever took place on my part or on the part of the Principal but the beatings and harassment continued, regardless. My third visit with the Principal would be my last as it was determined that I was taking up too much of their time. I was transferred to the care of the Guidance Counselor.

The Guidance Counselor always seemed distant, indifferent, and cold. There was an overwhelming sense that they didn't care for confrontation. We went to the first floor office- a blank, stale room with pale, standard, wooden chairs with straight backs. A clear, plain wooden table was in the middle of the room. They sat on one side with their notebook and pen and I sat on the other side looking around at the minimal decorations of educational posters sticky tacked to the walls. The Guidance Counselor asked me to reiterate my story so they could get the details from my perspective. They assured me that something would be done about the situation.

I was instructed to tell all of my teachers about what was going on and they would apprise them, as well, on their end.

One thing that became increasingly evident as I began to pick apart the Guidance Counselor when I was preparing to write this book, was that their body language was poor, and even that's being generous. As a seventh grader going through physical, verbal, and emotional abuse from classmates and ambivalence displayed by other teachers, I was not in the proper mindset (nor had I received the proper training) to assess body language. Hell, I couldn't even read my own body language at that point in time. The Guidance Counselor was always closed off. Some part of their body was always crossed or reaching for the door. If they were leaning forward taking notes they would cross their wrists when they were listening. Other times, when they were speaking, they would either have their arms crossed or ankles crossed as they leaned back in their chair. Then other times they would be speaking with me with their arms crossed and their leg would be stretched out to the side pointed directly to the door. The language they used also indicated that they were not enthusiastic about helping out. Their language was always focused on actions that *I* could take and things *I* could say and do to de-escalate or avoid abusive situations rather than how *we* could work *together* to be proactive and potentially stop the abusive behavior from happening. It almost felt like I was being blamed for all of this. Despite being in a leadership role, or at least a position a student should be able to turn to in times of trouble, the Guidance Counselor never seized the opportunity to take the lead to create an action plan, hold people accountable and responsible for their actions, set a deadline with measurable goals and actions, or at least bump it up to the Principal if they felt unable to properly handle the situation at their level, on their own. In short, it felt as if I was being interviewed or interrogated rather than being counseled, or helped.

It should be noted that, at this point in time "bullying" wasn't the buzzword that it is now. Georgia was the first state to pass an anti-bullying law in 1999[1]. The earliest mention of an anti-bullying law being passed in the Commonwealth of Massachusetts is the Anti-Bullying Act of 2010[2]. Social media wasn't a thing yet, either. Kids still handled their business with fistfights. Unfortunately, violence was condemned in my household and I was instructed never to fight under any circumstances. So I didn't. (Please note: I address this later in Part V: "Helping Others & Ourselves" under the chapter "Teaching Children to Defend Themselves." I think you know what direction I lean on that topic.

We have to remember that the world has evolved and changed so rapidly in recent years regarding our knowledge, education, understanding, and acceptance of mental health challenges. In the late 1990s the misinformation, public perception, and stigma still loomed large over anyone with a mental health diagnosis. Even learning disabilities like dyslexia were viewed as a black spot on a person, making them second-class citizens. Thankfully, people like Richard Branson, Daymond John, and Oprah Winfrey have risen to places of prominence in our society to dispel that misjudgment and to prove for others challenged with dyslexia that the challenge can be overcome. The stigma of mental health challenges during this time was set in the mindset of a lack of knowledge. If people (society as a whole) did not understand something, especially concerning mental health diagnoses, then whatever was unknown or misunderstood was automatically labeled as "bad" and should be ridiculed. If that mindset sounds familiar in present times, that's because it is, unfortunately. That mindset is still very prominent today. Despite more and more information becoming available,

---

[1] Bullying Laws. (n.d.). NoBullying.com. Retrieved from http://nobullying.com/category/bullying-facts/bullying-laws/
[2] Bullying Prevention and Intervention Resources. (n.d.). Massachusetts Department of Elementary and Secondary Education. Retrieved from http://www.doe.mass.edu/bullying/

mental health challenges are still widely misunderstood and the stigma is still alive and well.

Teen suicide wasn't heard of as prominently, either. When it did happen it was seen as reprehensible, shameful, and detestable. The community ignored it because they felt bad for the family and the parents didn't say anything because they felt they had failed as parents. The most common cause of death in those circumstances was, "they don't know what happened." I recall a young lady that lived in my neighborhood and went to my church who died by suicide. She was older than me and I remember the other kids in the church were asking for information about her and the church leaders simply explained that "She wanted to be with God." I think that aptly illustrates, simultaneously, the naivety of the church and the reluctance of the adults at the time to broach the topic in an intelligent and meaningful way with children or even amongst themselves. Teachers and school administrators still held the idiom, "boys will be boys" as a solid, legitimate reason not to intervene in cases of bullying, harassment, hazing, and abuse. It should also be noted that nothing was ever formally reported or documented in my case. I didn't record any dates, times, locations, or responses for people I spoke with. I simply trusted that they knew what steps needed to be taken and that they would do the right thing.

Losing My Compass

Monday, February 3, 1997 began as any other day but it ended as one that would directly change the course of my personal history. It was actually a good day. I didn't have gym- which meant I didn't get beat up, Leader and thefollowers behaved themselves, and I don't think I got any ridicule from any other students that day. My mom had the day off from work so she picked me up at 2 o'clock and we went home, as usual. I entered the house, shut off the alarm system, and tossed my book bag on my chair and went outside to retrieve the papers for my paper route. As I came back into the house my mom was listening with a wide eyed shock to a message on the answer machine. It was my uncle telling us to get to the hospital right away. She called him back on his cell phone and it was a series of "What happened?" Several okays, and "We'll be right over." She hung up the phone looked at me as I stood dead center in the foyer and said "Vô (Portuguese for "grandpa") is dead." I couldn't tell you anything else she said at that point. My body did what it wanted to do. I wasn't present. I wasn't in control. I raced to the couch and threw myself into the pillows, sobbing. She said several times that we had to go but I didn't want to do anything at that point.

My grandfather drove a black GMC pickup for many years. My grandmother had a Buick LeSabre that was on its last legs. That morning he had gone out looking at new cars for my grandmother. He settled on a Buick Century and was ready to buy it… with my grandmother's approval, of course. As he went to leave the dealership to get my grandmother he tried to go out the "In" door by pushing on it. The girl at the desk said, "Sir, you can't go out that way. You have to use the other door." He reportedly turned to her, said, "Leave it to me to do something so silly," smiled and immediately collapsed. One of the responding officers was a relatively young, newer cop that started CPR immediately upon arriving at the scene. He became close friends of the family because of the incident. During my internship with the local police department while in college, I had the privilege of riding with this officer. One day we started driving the back roads a bit and he opened up to me about that day. He was always very professional and I wanted to model myself after him if I ever had the opportunity to become a police officer. That afternoon he showed me a more human, vulnerable side of himself when he lamented not being able to do more for my grandfather on that fateful day. He vividly recounted how he could've taken a faster route, passed a few more cars, or acted faster when he arrived on the scene. What stands out in my mind was how demonstrative he became and how visibly angry, upset, and even shaken he became when talking about the ambulance ride. "Dammit! I had him alive in that ambulance! He was alive when he got to the hospital!"

My memory of the next few days are filled with vignettes and still frames of mourning and sadness. My grandmother's house filled with people, food, and flowers. My older cousin, who came up from Florida, teaching me how to tie a real tie properly in the basement of the funeral home just to give me a break from the grief of seeing the one person whom I could trust and count on lying unresponsive in a box surrounded by flowers at the wake. My younger cousins and I changing the date on the desk display in my grandfather's study to reflect the date of his death and writing a note professing our love and devotion to him. A few of my friends coming through the line at his wake and me not being able to put a whole sentence together to thank them for their support. My great uncle, my grandfather's brother, in the last stages of his fight with colorectal cancer, angrily swiping his hat off his seat at the closure of the wake the night before the funeral saying, "That should be me in that damn box!" My cousins and I walking with my grandmother down the street to the church behind his casket (an old Portuguese tradition). Members of the police honor guard and motorcycle escort openly crying as my grandfather's casket and our family filed by. The church being filled to standing room only and not a dry eye in the place. The funeral procession being rumored to be over a mile long and bringing the traffic in parts of the city to a complete halt.

New Weapons II

The most difficult part of this ordeal was when the beatings escalated a third time. They, the followers, discovered they could use their ties and belts as weapons. This came after one of the followers was hit with a belt as discipline at home. Many of the kids in my school, myself included, came from very conservative, Catholic, traditional old-school Portuguese households. Many of these households are made up of parents who immigrated to this country as children and grew up with the old world, "Motherland" values, insights, beliefs, and practices. One of these practices is corporal punishment. I know corporal punishment is now viewed as archaic, over-the-top, barbarian, and overkill in today's society but, as the voice of experience, there aren't many bad behaviors that a swift shot in the ass and a stern directive couldn't fix. Some of the people I have talked to about this who are my parents' age (who grew up in the late 1950s and into the 60s) told me tales of fear of being sent to the principal's office because they'd whoop the student for insubordination at the school and the student would go home and get whooped again for acting up in school. A friend of the family told me the rationale was, "If they had a good enough reason to whoop you at school, that's good enough reason for me, too!"

Whoopings came in all shapes and sizes. Sometimes the child would have to go out to the woods or down by the brook to pull the branch that they would get hit with. Other times it was the leather part of their dad's belt. Still others got the business end of their mother's shoes (usually with a nice thick wooden sole). I was fortunate that my mom usually favored an openhanded swat on my backside. However, I screwed up bad enough at my grandmother's house one day to warrant having to do some quick math on the fly. She took me down to her basement and pointed to a large wooden spoon and fork on the wall. She told me to pick which one I was going to get hit with. This became a trigonometry problem. Force equals mass times acceleration. The spoon was large and heavy: lots of mass but it's tough to get moving. The fork was a little lighter but the tines were longer and wider than the spoon. The deciding factor was the aerodynamics. The spaces in between the tines provided the aerodynamics that shifted the "acceleration" portion of the equation in the fork's favor. I definitely needed to choose the spoon to save my hide. Unfortunately, the followers didn't give me the courtesy of any options. They just tried everything they could get their hands on.

First, they tried belts. They grabbed the buckle in their hand and used it as a mid range whip, catching me with just the tip of the belt's fabric. This was more of a surprise than painful because it was unannounced, except for maybe a few snickers- but that could usher in any mischief- and unprovoked like all the attacks were. It was worse when they use the belts as a close range weapon where they would get me flat across the whole back with the entire length of the belt. This hurt more because, although it was less energy transferred, they got more coverage. The worst spot for this kind of attack was across the back of both knees. The instinctual reaction is to get the limb out of the striking zone but when both legs have that reaction my knees simply buckled and I collapsed to the ground. Thankfully, they only attempted the buckle end of the belt once. That approach worked *too well* and was too effective. I got hit in the middle of my back just below the shoulder blades. I quickly inhaled at the shock of the impact. I couldn't catch my breath and I lost my footing. I redlined. I was unable to function for several minutes. Even Leader and the followers couldn't get any enjoyment out of that. It was over too quickly for their liking.

They needed another way to get their point across. At first they grabbed the knot of their clip-on ties but the fabric didn't carry enough energy to produce a good enough impact. They slid pens into the hollow pocket in the back of the tie. That had a better effect but it was unreliable because the pen could fly out of the tie and hit one of their own. Who knew even bullies had to watch out for friendly fire?! When they flipped the tie around, they got their desired result. Unfortunately for me, they discovered they could do even more damage if they flipped the metal clip of the tie out. This created a fish hook effect which punctured, cut, and sliced me with every stroke. It was these instances- thankfully few in number- that resulted in me soaking my shirts when I got home from school due to the blood stains. The worst attack was when a left-hander was on my right side and a right-hander was on my left side. They were alternating hits that raked across my back and someone came running up behind me and delivered an overhead strike that left a shallow but painful cut from the nape of my neck just under the collar of my shirt to my lower back. I can't help but remember my arms reflexively jerking back, my face wrenching in agony, and my knees buckling from the shock which sent me crumpling to the ground in a heap. I covered my neck and head with my hands and I tried to make myself as small as possible and move as much as possible to try to evade the attack. I guess I let out a loud cry because the followers scattered to throw on their clothes quickly and encouraged me to get dressed faster, as well. When I got home I tried to take my shirt off to soak it but it was stuck to my back with dried blood. I hopped in the shower, turned it on as hot as I could stand it to dull the pain, and slowly pulled my shirt off my ripped back as I winced and groaned through gritted teeth. Then I soaked the shirt in the sink in the basement and went about my drum practice as if nothing was wrong. When I was questioned about the shirt I made up an accident in art class.

I think at this point it is important to note that I wasn't the only one to be treated this way. There was another boy in the seventh grade with me who was quite a bit taller than I was, a bit heavier, and a little more cumbersome than most of the kids in our grade. He didn't want to be cool. He didn't bother anyone. He only wanted to go to school, do his time, and go home. His crime: he was a big kid. His punishment: the same constant, incessant torture as me. He was pelted incessantly with insults, barbs, and jabs about his weight, appearance, and intellect. Admittedly, sometimes I was thankful when their attention was drawn away from me so I could have a day or two of peace, quiet, and an opportunity to relax a little bit. He was different than me, though. He was a fighter and he used his size to his advantage. I always admired him for standing up for himself like that. He was able to routinely take out two or three guys before the full group, the pack mentality, overpowered him.

The one incident that stood out to me regarding him was in eighth grade (please forgive the break in chronology) and the followers were feeling their oats. They were talking a good game but the big guy was ready. When they finally engaged, he easily dispatched the first two assailants but the other three started getting leverage. He began to tire quickly once the other two rejoined the fray and they began to maneuver him towards the shower- fully clothed in his school uniform. No matter how hard he fought to defend himself, I knew he was only prolonging the inevitable. I eventually heard the shower nozzle turn on, quickly followed by cheers of victory. As we walked out to our next class he heard the snickers, saw the pointed fingers and grins, and even saw the puzzled looks of teachers passing by who still said and did nothing. When we arrived at our next class the teacher instructed him to get a new uniform from the office but the followers and Leader received no disciplinary action because he wouldn't give their names and I knew better than to open my mouth. Otherwise the same treatment and more would surely befall me.

I couldn't figure out why the followers liked to pick on the other guy for the life of me. They knew they were going to win. Then it hit me- that was exactly the point. Even though they couldn't take him down individually they knew that they'd eventually overpower him all together. They saw it as a challenge. How far could they get individually before they had to call in the reinforcements? From an observer's vantage point, this appeared to be similar to a canned hunt on a big game preserve. A large trophy animal is placed in a designated area of the game park to be tracked down and "harvested" by someone for their collection. It's an unfair hunt with the circumstances greatly shifted in favor of the hunter. Similarly, it was the same "stacked deck" mentality employed in the locker room. It was like watching the young adolescents of a lion pride haphazardly take down an unsuspecting wildebeest. The young lions have no clue what they're doing but their sheer numbers overpower and inundate the wildebeest.

Coach II

After my grandfather's death I was broken, shattered, and emotionally unavailable. I had checked out as much as possible. Leader saw this and knew it was a show of weakness. He and the followers took advantage of my vulnerability and their abuse was amplified. They used my loss as a psychological weapon and they increased the severity and frequency of the physical abuse. They began to stretch the harassment outside of the locker room, as well. It became a game of skill to see who could hit me the most times with spitballs in class. I know it was a competition because I was proudly shown the scorecard. I remember one class, specifically, that they were particularly incessant. I remember tapping the girl in front of me on the shoulder and telling her it would be wise to put her long hair inside her sweater because I didn't want her becoming collateral damage just because I was the main target.

I remembered what Coach had said about needing fresh evidence in order to take any action. Every time they broke my skin or hit me hard enough to cause a bruise or a welt I got dressed as quickly as possible and went to find Coach. When I found Coach he would either dismiss what I showed him as insufficient- especially the bruises, because those were explained away by my participation in the class- or he was too busy working on something else and couldn't be bothered to check.

As time passed and the beatings intensified, I clearly remember running up the stairs and calling to Coach in various degrees of undress trying to gain his attention to "witness" the abuse. Oddly enough, no matter how loud I screamed he never heard me. The most egregious example of this was when I was subjected to a round of tie clip scourging that pushed me past the point of taking action. I put on my pants and shoes, grabbed my book bag, gathered the rest of my clothes in my arms, and went up to the bottom landing to call up to Coach. When he didn't respond I moved to the next landing and called louder. That didn't work either, so I moved up to the last landing and yelled out to Coach to come see me. When I didn't receive a response from him I made the decision to force his hand. I went all the way up to the top and stood in the doorway bare-chested, shirt and tie in one hand, gym bag in the other and screamed Coach's full name at him. When he realized my state of undress he quickly leapt off the stage and started motioning for me to go down the stairs back to the locker room. I told him to look at my back which was obviously scratched up and I turned around. He reiterated that I had to go downstairs to finish changing or I would receive a detention for insubordination. When I told him I had fresh evidence of the abuse he told me that anything I said or showed him didn't matter because it was done while breaking the rules. It was now official, Coach was against me and I needed to look for help elsewhere.

Equal Opportunity Abuse

What I got physically from the guys I got equally as bad from the girls, verbally and emotionally. As someone quite nebbishy, I found it difficult to talk to girls- as one could imagine with all this bullying going on. Aside from the fact that my reputation preceded me, my fear of rejection pushed my anxiety far into overdrive. Of course, in a popularity driven, "you are who you hang out with" social environment, very few people wanted to be around me. The idea of being guilty by association was a very real thing with quite obvious, real, physical consequences. I recall writing a lengthy, verbose, and heartfelt letter to a young lady who caught my attention in 7th grade. I typed it out using a script font (to appear elegant and romantic, of course) and I signed it "Your Secret Admirer." Well, by the end of homeroom (which was the first "class" of the day) my cover was blown and the "secret" was all over the school... as well as her response, a resounding "NO!" I still don't think I've lived that moment down amongst a small, close knit group of friends. Sometimes I would've preferred the physical beat down compared to the emotional barbs of the girls. It's one thing to get your ass handed to you by a bunch of guys. That's animalistic, that's in our DNA to some extent. Sure, it can hurt but it's over and done with in a matter of minutes. But to receive the cold shoulder from a whole grade's population of girls was difficult. That goes against the biological script- no girl means no mate. No mate means no offspring. No offspring and my family tree is a stump. Sure it may sound overdramatic and sensationalized now, but we were all teenagers once (or still are) and know that statement seems all too real when we're in the throes of the hormonal hurricane called puberty.

I remember the looks, the snickers, and the jabs that came from anonymous voices in a crowd of girls. I had notes written on my papers when they were handed back. Sometimes my name was crossed out and "Secret Admirer" was written in its place. I did have a girlfriend in sixth grade. Well, at least a friend that happened to be a girl, but we spent a lot of time together. Early in seventh grade I noticed that she hung out with the girls more often. The more she hung out with the girls the less my notes and phone calls were received or replied to. Slowly, the rate of calls and the notes dwindled, then they ended. I eventually caught on that what we had was no more.

Nightmares/
Night Terrors

As the bullying progressed I began to have more and more
restless nights or nights where I got no sleep at all. I had
difficulty sleeping because I was reliving and replaying
conversations and scenarios in my head. I would play them
through, figuring out how it was *my* fault and what *I* could
have done differently (just like the Guidance Counselor
instructed me to do). Maybe I could have ignored them, or
said something different, or I don't know, maybe even stand
up for myself and defend myself. I would wake up in tears and
my bed sheets would be strewn about from an obvious attempt
to defend myself in my nightmare. Sometimes I would wake
up in a cold sweat sitting straight up, jaunted for my sleep by
something that startled me so much in my dreamscape that I
felt I must wake up and defend myself in real life. I was also
challenged by- actually, reflecting on the situation now, I'll
confidently say "suffered from"- night terrors. Night terrors
are unrealistic, horrid, dark visions. Mine happened to be of
destruction, torture, and death. Often the same vision would
loop throughout the night or morph into a flight of equally
unrealistic proportions out of the hellish dreamscape. Often, as

the nightmare would appear to enter into a happier place of consolation or relief, it would be time to wake up. Looking back, this makes sense that the brightness and levity of the dream came as the sun started shining through my bedroom drapes. This interrupted pattern of sleep or sleeplessness started to negatively affect my ability to function in school and at home.

Most of these dreams were in black and white. One dream in particular was of a revolutionary battle scene where the attacking good guys were being bombarded by enemies in plain sight on a small hill. No matter how many shots the charging army took they couldn't land a single shot and they were being destroyed by the dozen by canons and Gatling guns. Then they charged on further, but when they reached the foot of the hill the ground gave way to reveal a large pit surrounding the hill filled with large wooden pikes. As the attacking forces charged the hill they fell into the pit, impaling themselves on the pikes. The attackers wouldn't stop running into this pit and the pit never got filled or clogged with bodies. It was a perpetual cycle of gore and death. I'm no dream specialist but I believe that this was representative of how I felt with my attackers. No matter how hard I tried, who I talked to, or what I did they were fortified in plain sight and I couldn't touch them. I felt no choice but to continue running at them to at least *try* to stop them but I was easily thwarted time after time. For the longest time, longer than I can trace back, I have had dreamless sleep- or at least dreams I could not recall in the morning. Any attempt to explain this would merely be a stretch to grasp at a loose understanding of dreams, dreaming, and how the sleeping mind works. I recently started to have dreams again, and I would be lying if this wasn't by design and the result of difficult, diligent preparation and work.

In the book *Think and Grow Rich,* Napoleon Hill presents the concept of immediacy. This concept plays on the law of attraction where the brain works to formulate plans to achieve and acquire whatever it is fed. The idea is to consistently feed the brain a set of goals and equations to work on. It was only when I started to feed my brain specific goal-themed topics that I began to have dreams again. They started sparsely at first, but as I have continued to improve on this practice over the past months, the results of fruitful dreams have increased in frequency, complexity, and detail.

Lack of sleep can play some pretty nasty tricks on the body and mind. When we consider this interruption of the normal sleep cycle and resting behavior was in a time of great hormonal upheaval and imbalances, it's evident that I certainly had some challenges on my hands. I wasn't hungry at the appropriate times, so my meals were sometimes small. When I did eat I would scavenge through the cupboards and cabinets for anything appetizing. At this point my life, this category was reserved for ice cream and junk food. My lack of sleep at night meant a lack of energy in the classroom. This led to me being less than attentive (even to the point of occasionally not wanting to write in class- choosing, rather, to just completely zone out) which gained the ire of some of my teachers.

Think of a time when you were very tired (some of us may not have to dig too deep). What are the symptoms of being tired? Lethargy, irritability, poor communication skills, and poor coping mechanisms are all on the list. This doesn't sound like a list of qualities and characteristics that are fun to be around. Relationships were difficult for me to handle due to the sleeplessness and puberty. I felt the desire and need to be close to people but I didn't want to get too close for fear of being hurt *and* I was simply a bear to be around.

Why "Kill Yourself" Made Sense

Preparing for this book, I had to figure out where the idea of dying by suicide first entered my lexicon- where that idea came from, specifically. Upon deep thought and reflection of the first time I heard that phrase, I felt as if a black tide enveloped me in negativity. I had prepared myself well for this exercise, or at least I thought I did. I hadn't been in that headspace in a very long time. Even entering that mindset from an observational perspective and for analytical purposes was daunting and quite frightening. I needed to conjure that memory and those feelings up in order to neutralize that memory, address that skeleton, and stack it in the back of the closet, evaluating it along the way in order to help others.

We were in the locker room changing after gym class and they got me good (Raise your hand if you're surprised... didn't think so). I think it was during the belt stage because I remember redlining, just being totally incapacitated and gasping for breath. One of the followers- someone I couldn't identify now if it were a matter of life and death - put his book bag down right next to my face, stepped over my curled up body, bent down, and quietly said "Why don't you just fucking kill yourself and make this all go away?" Then he slapped me upside my head, and left the locker room. When I heard that phrase uttered to me the first time I was in a mental state where I felt like I was in a pitch dark room searching for the door handle. I was trying everything I could think of, speaking to anyone I felt might be able to lend any semblance of assistance, and getting nowhere regardless how diligent and steadfast my attempts to get help were. I felt like a cartoon character running full speed on ice because I was exhausting all my energy but not making any progress.

"Just fucking kill yourself" resonates with me because of the minimization of the action. The nonchalance and offhandedness of the remark floors me. Until that thought was placed in my head it wasn't an option. I had never thought of suicide until that moment. Where was his head? I wonder how he learned about suicide or how he came to the conclusion that it was a suitable bookend for my situation. What was he going through that it was so readily on his mind as an acceptable alternative to deal with my situation?

Even though this belongs in Part V: Helping Others & Ourselves, I'll mention it here. When other people dump nastiness on us- like this kid dumping "kill yourself" on me- we have to wonder what's going on In their lives that they aren't handling and they're projecting onto us. When people engage in behavior like this they are usually projecting inner turmoil and what they're saying has nothing to do with us, we're just an available target to unload on.

But, the suggestion made sense because it was an option I knew would work. I wouldn't have to deal with Leader or his followers. I wouldn't have to deal with teachers and administrators who obviously couldn't be bothered to help me. Perhaps losing me would bring attention to the issue and assist other kids that were going through similar situations. Maybe someone would pay attention to me after I was gone. Those thoughts and words were all going through my head within milliseconds after the follower uttered those words to me. They would haunt me for over 18 years.

I remember dwelling on the subject of suicide, sudden stops to life (like airplane crashes, car accidents, drowning, getting hit by a bus, or any other kind of accident), and wonder what it feels like. What does it take to get to the point of no return, then keep going? I wondered if the proverbial lights just go out, if there's such a thing as an out of body experience, and, most importantly, what happens afterwards. I was concerned what would happen in the physical world as well as spiritual. Growing up Catholic (I'm still a practicing Catholic but I've opened my belief system to include more influences- sought a second opinion, if you will [more like a few dozen opinions],) I was taught that, since suicide is murdering oneself and murder is a cardinal sin- the most serious kind of sin- the perpetrator (also the victim, in this case) would not be allowed into Heaven. In fact, for the longest time Catholics who died by suicide were not allowed to have a funeral mass, the Rite of Christian Burial. Thankfully, in the early 2000s, the Vatican formally lightened its stance on suicide. Although Catholics who died by suicide were allowed to be buried from the church for quite some time, there was still strong language in church doctrine condemning the act.

Though the church certainly does not condone suicide by any stretch of the imagination and the act is still condemned as an act of violence towards oneself, the church's viewpoint of mental health has matured and has become less constricting. Basically, in order to commit a sin we have to be of sound mind. In the instance of suicidal thoughts and the action of suicide, the person is not of sound mind and therefore can't be held accountable or responsible for their actions. As such, the church believes that God forgives them for their actions and welcomes them into Heaven. I address this subject deeper much later in an exploration of the view different religions have on accepting and condoning mental health care as well as their specific views on suicide in An Exploration of Faith & Mental Health. As much as this comforted me, I wasn't ready or willing to risk it. When I speak with my clients about leveraging or manipulating their Breaking Point to leave their Comfort Zone in order to achieve their desired results and their goals, it's a tedious, painstaking, often slow and steady buildup of confidence, trust, anxiety, momentum, and energy before a sharp, sudden burst of action where they are almost unconscious as they are overcoming obstacles, defeating challenges, and achieving results far beyond their perceived limitations. This also happens with negative thoughts and actions, too, such as suicide. I am grateful and thankful that my breaking point was not leveraged or manipulated enough to drive me to the point of no return.

Addictions

When we are faced with difficult situations, especially ones that last a substantial amount of time, we often find ourselves seeking comfort, an escape, or a release of pent-up anxiety, stress, energy, and anger. In these moments we are looking for coping mechanisms in our environment or network and seeking sources of strength. I am no different. I was no different. The truth is that the combination of my coping mechanisms- some still faults, others still my strengths- kept me alive. I fear that if I didn't purge my mind and body regularly of the negativity that was rotting me away from the inside out, I wouldn't be here today.

My faith has been a big part of my life and it was instilled in me at a young age. I had observed most of my family being very involved with the church. My grandfather was a lector (reader), collector, Eucharistic Minister, and a CCD (Sunday school) teacher. My grandmother was a Eucharistic Minister, CCD teacher, attended daily mass, and helped around the church office on a regular basis. My mom was a lector, Eucharistic Minister, and CCD teacher. So it was only fitting that I started as an altar server the week after I received my First Communion in second grade.

Around the sixth grade the deacon and priest started allowing me to partake in the sacramental wine on a regular basis- just a small sip of consecrated wine from the community chalice that was shared among the people on the altar: the priest, deacon, lector, Eucharistic Ministers, and the altar servers. I recall enjoying the taste and the little "tingle" that it gave me. I quickly learned that if I positioned myself last in the line I was allowed to finish what was left in the chalice and get a bigger share. Also, part of my duties as an altar server was to prepare the altar for the next Mass. That meant getting the Portuguese sacramental (the book with the readings) placed on the lectern (the podium where the readings take place) and fill the flagons (the little glass vessels) full of water and wine respectively. As the abuse in school started to grow more intensely during seventh grade, I began the practice of rushing back to the sacristy after mass to replace the cross or candle I was carrying, rushing out to the altar to retrieve the flagons from the side altar, and hurrying to the sink to fill the wine as quickly as possible. Then I would take one or two large gulps of wine before filling the water and returning the flagons to the small table placed in the middle of the main aisle of the church. [If any priests are reading this, please consider this my confession. Forgive me, Father, for I have sinned.]

This practice carried over to home, as well. My parents were never ones to over indulge in alcohol and I've never seen them smoke. I seldom saw my dad drink a beer and very rarely saw my mom have a glass of wine. So, when my mom noticed a once unopened bottle of wine from the back of the refrigerator almost completely gone it raised some eyebrows. When we were preparing for a holiday dinner at our house and they opened the dry sink (where my parents kept the wine and liquor) to find all the wines (two or three bottles) had disappeared and half the bottle of Absolut vodka had mysteriously "evaporated" they knew something was up and I knew the party was over. I was told to smarten up and that I should know better than to get into stuff that wasn't meant for me. For most, this would've been a challenge to find more creative ways to get their fix, but this was enough to deter me from any further alcoholic adventures. My reasons for stopping were simple: I didn't want to disobey my parents and it became too much effort. In my adolescent mind I technically never *disobeyed* my parents because they never told me "no alcohol" before. (Yes, this is a common sense thing; however I think we can agree that common sense doesn't tend to be so common in the adolescent mind.) Also, they had started to institute new checks and balances- bottles were now routinely marked and checked.

It will come as no surprise that writing has been a welcomed reprieve from reality for a great deal of my life. I attribute much of my vivid imagination, expansive vocabulary, and attention to detail in my writing to my time studying the smallest details of movement, shading, the environment, and texture during this time of my life. I focused on the minutia of what interested me (which lived in my imagination) in order to avoid the magnitude of what disgusted and appalled me in real life. I also wrote letters. I wrote a lot of letters: letters that were never sent, never delivered, and never received. Writing was a way for me to say what I wanted to say, to whom I wanted to say it, and how I wanted to say it without any responsibility or accountability for my thoughts or words. I could express my true anger, frustrations, concerns, and confusion without the fear of judgment, retribution, or punishment. I could express my true passion, adoration, care, and frustrations without worrying about the incessant mocking and badgering. Writing allowed me to create a world to escape to and write myself in as the king of my domain. I pictured how I could defend myself like an action hero: instantly and miraculously knowing and employing skills with proficiency in the martial arts, firearms, and other means of getting out of tight spots unscathed.

One practice that I developed for writing in school was to use two notebooks. I had one notebook that was solely dedicated to taking notes in each individual class and one notebook dedicated to my doodles, musings, journal entries, poems, stories, character development, and anything else that popped in my mind. At the end of our 8th grade yearbook the editing team projected me to be a poet and couldn't imagine me not writing poetry. I had a method to my madness with that notebook, as well. At least once in every class the teacher asked to see what I was working on. I showed them my class notes- which they weren't too concerned with because I continued to be a decent student- and I presented my other notebook to them face up, not where I was currently writing. Sometimes I would even offer to show them my new material after class so they didn't think I was hiding anything from them. My secret was that in the front of the notebook I had all my sappy, lovey-dovey poems. I wrote about the girls I liked, or a cool tree with fire red foliage I recently saw, or a short story about a cute puppy playing with the kids. I showed off the nice, cute, and friendly stuff willingly. In the back of the notebook I wrote the hurtful, painful things. Letters to my aggressors, poems and lyrics about hurt, abandonment, rejection, lack of support, lack of trust, loneliness, and suicide. When I would start crying out of hopelessness and the weight of the negativity that was coursing through my thoughts and body I just flipped to a poem about my grandfather and say I was just missing him. My teachers knew me as a super emotional, sensitive kid so it was a plausible and easily passable excuse.

The most important and most therapeutic addiction I have developed has been drumming. Drumming was my true release valve and my savior in middle school. Every day I would get home as quickly as possible, change out of my uniform as quickly as possible (stopping only to soak my shirt if I got blood on it), and practice until supper. My parents would flash the basement lights to let me know when supper was ready. After supper I would practice again until it was time to do my homework. I still keep the same rule that I don't drum before 9am or after 9pm for the sake of my neighbors' sanity. I became obsessive about drums and learning everything I could about them and their music because I knew if I didn't immerse myself in this world of music I would more than likely end up hurting others… or myself. I surrounded myself with drum education books, magazines, videos, and anything I could get my hands on. I studied rudiments, foot technique, and ambidexterity- that means leading with both hands. Then I became obsessed with showmanship and I started studying how to spin the sticks, do tricks, and how to get faster at everything I did. What drew me to drums (and still drives me today) is that a drummer will never truly master the drums. A true drummer, a true professional in *any* realm, actually, will always be learning and always be working on improving something. There is no "best" drummer because there are so many styles and nuances. But most of all, the drumming community is easily the most accepting, strongest community amongst musicians. We may argue the finer points of Neil Peart, Buddy Rich, Lars Ulrich, Travis Barker, Dennis Chambers, and Tony Royster, Jr but at the end of the day we're all content to be men and women who find joy and solidarity in hitting things with sticks to make noise in rhythm.

Sexual Orientation

Sexual orientation came into question when I started writing. It was "gay" to express your emotions through poetry, especially positive or romantic emotions. Actually, come to think of it, it was "gay" to do anything that the cool kids determined wasn't cool. When I pointed out that their favorite song lyrics were poetry, they quickly silenced me and defended my observation by saying those writings were coupled with amazing music. They were never able to provide a solid timeline where "the faggot writing poetry in middle school" turned into "the music or literary genius worthy of a young boy's praise and idolization." It sure wasn't in any of the books I read and none of the adults I asked had a clue, either. I couldn't help but question my own sexuality. It's called the law of repetition. When a thought or idea is forced upon us constantly over a long period of time we find ways to convince ourselves of its merit. If we hear something enough times we start to believe it, and hell, nothing else made sense at that point, why should something as complex as my sexuality be clear? I remember thinking, "How can I be gay? How can I be a fag if the people I think of when I write these poems or lyrics are girls?" The math didn't compute but that didn't stop me from questioning myself. I mean, they *are* cool kids, they should know. Maybe I gave off a vibe that I didn't even know about.

As I have grown older, even before I started working on my deeper mental health challenges, this always bothered me greatly. Why... How has being homosexual morphed into being less than respectable or even become a derogatory term? Hell, if you compared me to the likes of Elton John, Freddie Mercury, or the man that has stepped in for Mercury with Queen, Adam Lambert, I would accept those as amazing compliments (though, please don't ask me to sing). Likewise, I would kill to have Harvey Fierstein's voice, and an ounce of his creativity and artistic ability. I fear that this topic deserves a book- actually several- dedicated to it.

I firmly believe that many aspects of our world- race, sexual orientation, learning style, political leanings, and taste in music to name a few- more closely resemble a color palette rather than the dichotomous perception of black and white. I'm exploring the idea of putting these musings and research together in a project that explores and explains how civilizations were constructed- that is, pieced together to serve a greater purpose (which shouldn't be read or translated as "a greater good")- and illustrate how we can employ this information to improve our own lives. After all, those who do not learn from the past are doomed to repeat it.

The Plan & The Letter

I knew when, where, how, and why I'd take my own life. I had a plan in place. I had done my research and planned everything to the smallest detail. Originally, I didn't want to include any details of my plan because I feared giving people any ideas. Upon reflection, I quickly realized that the information and resources were out there for me in the Web 1.0 era (before social media) so I'd be naïve to think they aren't available anymore. More importantly, I hope that if anyone reading this is seeking ways to harm themselves that they call the National Suicide Prevention Lifeline (1-800-273-8255), get in touch with someone in their support network, or look for my email or phone number first so they can get in touch and get ahead of whatever is impacting their lives. Oh, and look no further: AJ@CrushComplacency.com.

In the spirit of full disclosure, this was my plan. I had seen the picture of the co-conspirators that were involved in President Abraham Lincoln's assassination after they were hanged. I figured that hanging may be the easiest way to dispatch myself. I looked up hanging on the web browser (Google wasn't a glimmer in Larry Page's and Sergey Brin's eyes at this point) and instead of information on the Lincoln co-conspirators I was provided detailed and elaborate information on the art of hanging. (Though gruesome and dark, there *is* a fine art to it.) Curiosity got the better of me and I found out that prisoners habitually used the reinforced hem of a bed sheet most often to do the deed. I can attest from my time as a correction officer that this is true. The website gave the drop height ratio for various weights and even details on the various types of knots that are used. It was frightening and fascinating that so much thought and time went into something so dark.

My plan was to wait until night. I would slip out of the far side of my bed, tear the seam of my sheet and start working on the noose. After the noose was complete I would retrieve my letter (we'll get to that in a minute) and place it carefully on my pillow. Then, I'd go into my closet, clear the front pole of clothes, secure the noose to the pole, stand on two of my storage totes, and fall backwards.

I have to impress upon everyone that this was a *very, extremely* poor plan. One sobering thought I found in my research is that most people who attempt hanging don't perish due to the drop- they die due to asphyxiation, or lack of oxygen to the brain. It's not quick and easy, there's usually a lot of pain and struggle that goes with it. I was all set with pain- that was a deal breaker for me. I like certainty. This plan was a lot of things, certain was not one of them.

I also wrote a note. Well, actually a letter. Honestly, I wrote many suicide letters, many good bye letters. I made edits and adjustments in a constant effort to word things perfectly (shocker that I was a perfectionist about my writing, I know). I had good days or weeks when I would read the letter and tear it up. I always kept the latest draft in a secure place because I never knew when I would need it. I always kept a notebook by my bed. It was my drumset when I couldn't play the drums. If there was noise in my head- that is, negative, painful, pounding thoughts or images- I would write them out. I would write until the thoughts were gone and I was fully exhausted. Now, I'm happy to report that I again have a notebook by my bed. However, now it is used to capture ideas that wake me up due to inspiration, not desperation.

The idea of out of body experiences played to my empathetic and sensitive side. I envisioned every aspect of the process. Who would find me? How would they react? What would they think of the note? I hope they would know it wasn't their fault. Damn, who was I kidding? They'll blame themselves. Hell, how would my grandmothers react? My aunt and uncle? My cousins? Wow, I never imagined that before. I envisioned my wake. What would happen to my body? Would they need to do an autopsy? I wonder what embalming entails. What would my parents dress me in? God, I hope not that horrid camel hair jacket. I saw former teachers, family members, friends of the family, my parents' coworkers, my paper route customers, baseball teammates and coaches, and people from the church community all coming to pay their respects and support my family.

Then my attention focused on my mom. Man, she'd be destroyed. Fun fact: I'm not an only child. I had an older brother that was brought to full term and was stillborn. How could I justify the actions I took to myself or anyone I may have to answer to on the other side? I became very self conscious, even guilty that I had these thoughts of giving up. *Really dude, she's been by your side the whole way and you're going to back out when times get tough? You haven't even been able to talk with her about this!* Even in those, my darkest days, I was an empathetic people pleaser. My (nearly) fatal flaw was that I wanted others to be happy, even at my own expense. Sure, I was contemplating making some people happy but was I going to make the *right* people happy?

Pursuit of ~~Happiness~~

Happiness is a term and concept that has dumbfounded me for a long time. It's one of those sloppy, formless, subjective terms that morphs from one person to another and continually transform throughout our lives. As I have explored the proverbial rabbit hole of the concept of happiness a strange thing happened. Many of us, myself included, accept happiness at face value. We accept *most* of our emotions and feelings at face value, actually. In fact, I'll go a step further and say that a lot of people aren't even consistently cognizant of their current mood. Happy is defined as, "Feeling or showing pleasure or contentment.[3]" I don't think that floats my boat. In *The Skeleton Key* (a personal development book I'm concurrently working on), I devote two chapters to the concept of being addicted to complacency. Contentment is listed as a synonym for complacency. With this in mind, and my disenchantment with mediocrity and complacency, I set out to find the next level of happiness. The "Pursuit of Happiness," by definition and exploration, now meant the "Pursuit of Complacency" or "Pursuit of Baseline/ Average." Don't get

[3] Happy. 2015. In OxfordDictionaries.*com*. Retrieved August 18, 2015, from http://www.oxforddictionaries.com/us/definition/american_english/happy

me wrong, when we're having a crappy day "happy" can seem like it's a long way off. However, to pursue average on a daily basis strikes me as a waste of time and energy (the two most precious commodities in the world). I'm not happy (read: content) when I'm average. I want excellence, superlative, extraordinary.

This is where our language gives us away. If we settle for average vocabulary and speak to a baseline level of accomplishment and productivity, then that is what our brain and our body will give us. When we expect more from ourselves and prime our brain to produce a superior product, then it will force our body to rise to the challenge. I challenge us all to answer the call and join the Pursuit of Ecstasy. Ecstasy is defined as an "Overwhelming feeling of great happiness or joyful excitement.[4]" Compare the synonyms of happy (content, complacent) to the likes of euphoria, jubilation, and exultation. Now *that* is a next level word!

The Pursuit of Ecstasy is different from the Pursuit of Happiness (and I believe it's what our Founding Fathers truly meant in the Declaration of Independence) in that we must work hard and take risks in order to achieve ecstasy. Happiness is a regular-season win. Ecstasy is the World Series. Happiness is collecting a consistent paycheck. Ecstasy is busting our butts to achieve financial abundance. Happiness is being of average health and average ability. Ecstasy is having the body we've always desired and the ability to do things we dreamed about. Happiness is the life that we have now. Ecstasy is the life we dream about having.

---

[4] Ecstasy. 2015. In OxfordDictionaries.*com*. Retrieved August 18, 2015, from http://www.oxforddictionaries.com/us/definition/american_english/ecstasy

The Ugly Truth

I have never told the full story of what happened in middle
school. I have shared parts of this story with a very small
number of people to varying degrees, but this is my first time
telling all of the details- even those that I am not proud of.
One aspect of the story I have never shared is something that I
am deeply embarrassed about and even ashamed of. I was in
the basement after school, as usual. Before I got to the area
that had my drum set, I stumbled across an orange electrical
cord that was left unraveled across the basement floor. I
picked up the cord with the intention of wrapping it up and
placing it back in my dad's toolbox. As I was wrapping the
cord around my left forearm I was struck by curiosity. I held
onto the end with the prongs- the "male" end- and measured
out a fair amount of cord, perhaps a full arm's wingspan and
brought my hands together to create a large loop. Then with
my left hand I made a smaller loop starting at the point I
measured out- half with cord I measured, half made of the
remaining cord- big enough to hold a basketball. I grabbed the
two pieces of wire together and started loosely wrapping the
cord I had measured out over the two pieces of cord towards
the loop. Then I fed the male connector back through the loops
and tighten the knot- a slipknot. I had fastened a noose.

I don't know where this fascination with nooses derived but I developed a habit of tying anything I could get my hands on into a noose. I would often tie string, rope, solder, and cords into nooses. Usually, I would make only a few loops in order to pass the creation off as a lasso if I was ever questioned about it. A few times my dad caught me and questioned me about it but I brushed it off as no big deal. I was just bored and it was "just a thing."

Only this time it almost wasn't "just a thing." I had occasionally put my creation around my neck and even tightened it as tight as I could stand a few times. I was curious about what it would feel like to be in that position: on the gallows, rope pulled tight against my neck, pulled upright so the knot is right in line with my cervical spine, then the trapdoor falls away, I gasp as I lose my footing... but then what? My dad was fixing one of the kitchen chairs because it was shaky. I grabbed it and placed it under the oil pipe- the thickest, sturdiest pipe in the basement. I got on the chair with the electrical cord noose draped around my neck. I threw the cord over the pipe and wrapped it around two or three times. I dressed the noose's knot to the back of my skull and pulled out the slack from the portion wrapped around the pipe. Then I pulled the knot down snug to my neck, tighter than I can recall doing it before. It was so tight that merely bending my knees made it difficult to breathe.

My dad has always had a habit of having many projects going at one time. As an electronics and computer networking instructor at the local regional vocational technical high school he would routinely have a stereo, computer, (at this point in time) VCRS, and a few other devices around the house being fixed for students, neighbors, or fellow teachers. He always loved to help others by fixing what he could. He often told the people he served that he was paid in Dunkin' Donuts gift cards- not surprisingly we'd go months without buying a cup of coffee out of our own pocket. While he provided a great service for people we knew, this meant that something had to give. Projects around the house didn't get done as quickly as they should have. The kitchen chair hadn't been fixed yet. In a sudden jolt, one of the legs became dislodged and the chair fell apart. I flailed my arms to attempt to catch my balance, I gasped as I lost my footing.

The answer to "… but then what?" is darkness. What happened was a blur, or more appropriately, a flash. It was as if a light bulb had exploded; a brilliant, sharp explosion of light followed by pitch darkness. I can't tell you what happened but the next thing I remember I was on the floor unable to breathe. In a wide eyed panicked I had one goal- find the problem. I grabbed at my throat and felt the cord digging into my neck, suffocating me like an anaconda on a National Geographic special. Problem identified. New mission: find a solution. As I worked, I kept trying to get air into my lungs. My diaphragm and lungs knew what to do but the circuit was literally closed off, unable to complete the command. I grasped the cord and worked my fingers between the cord and my neck. As I slipped my hand toward my left ear I remembered a sobering fact: most people hanged don't die from the fall, they expire due to asphyxiation- lack of oxygen to the brain. I simultaneously yanked on the cord and attempted to inhale- nothing. Wrong side- this was the "wrap" side that led to the knot, not the straight side that led to freedom. Milliseconds passed like hours as I slid my right hand under the cord and my left hand up to the knot. Kicking and flailing as I fought for my next breath, I remembered that movement uses energy and energy requires oxygen- something I had precious little of at the moment. I closed my eyes and stopped kicking. As my right hand reached just under my right ear and my left thumb and forefinger wrapped around the last loop of the knot closest to my head, I pulled in opposite directions three times as hard as I could muster.

Those first few breaths felt like a miracle that rejuvenated my body. My eyesight cleared, my body warmed up as newly oxygenated blood rushed to replenish my system and remove wasteful carbon dioxide from my body. As breathing became a normal commodity, again, I moved and writhed as I regained my strength. Then the emotions came. I was free to feel fear, pain, exasperation, elation, panic, and a host of other emotions. When something like that happens often times the brain doesn't know how to react, so it does everything. I laughed as I cried and cried as I looked around the room in wide eyed amazement and disbelief at what had just occurred. As homeostasis returned and I lay on my back simply grateful to be alive, I had a moment of shock- dad was on his way home at any minute.

When panic sets in routine goes by the boards. I quickly got to my feet and brushed myself off. I looked around and saw the basement in complete disarray. I put the chair back together as best as I could and replaced it at dad's workstation. Then, I gathered the electrical cord, untied the noose, and quickly wrapped it up as best as I could. I tidied up the basement a little more and concluded that it was in good enough condition to pass the eye test. I made my way upstairs and ripped open my book bag. Hurriedly, I made my way to the dining room table, flipped the book open to my homework assignment (I always bookmarked the page with a piece of paper or the handout to save time) and I got to work. Soon after I heard my father's truck pull in the driveway, then the back door being unlocked, then his keys and pocket protector filled with pens, an X-acto knife, and a small ruler were tossed onto the kitchen table, then his lunch bag being tossed onto the counter in the pantry. I watched him out of the corner of my eye as he stopped abruptly as he exited the pantry. He loosened his tie and unbuttoned his top button as he inquired, "No drums today? That's not like you." I looked up and stared blankly out the back window. Oh my God, I screwed up. In my panic I forgot it was still afternoon, not after supper. When panic sets in routine goes by the boards. In my panic I had broken my routine and he nailed it. Did he suspect anything? "Nah, just changing things up a bit. I want to get my homework done while the stuff is fresh in my head... And the Red Sox are playing the Mariners. I want to watch Griffey play." He responded with a simple "OK," as he headed upstairs to change.

Did I want to kill myself? I mean, I say it was an accident. I feel and believe that it was an accident. I say I was just being curious about the process and how it felt, but let's be honest, we can do a lot of things with ropes and electrical cords. They're both very useful for various things. However, a noose isn't one of those helpful things. A 13-year-old boy shouldn't know how to tie a noose, never mind how to tie one quickly and proficiently. However, on that day, in that time, I willfully and mindfully tied that electrical cord into a noose, put it around my neck, draped it over the heating pipe, and tightened it to the point it was uncomfortable. Did I want to kill myself? I don't believe so, but in that time I'm curious- I wonder if I would have been OK if it had happened. What happened in that basement that day is not normal, healthy, or appropriate behavior for 13 year-old, or for anyone. However, I'm here. Somehow, someway, I'm present and accounted for.

If you're at a point like this, whether in curiosity or you have more of a specific intention with a specific goal- I'll just say it- if you're contemplating suicide or thinking about taking your own life please put down this book. Please either pick up the phone or head to the computer (let's be honest, you probably have everything on your phone, anyways). Please call me at 508-465-5252 or e-mail me at AJ@CrushComplacency.com so we can work together, figure out where this is coming from, and get you to the proper people who can provide you with the professional, empathetic, and caring help that you need and deserve. Another great resource is the National Suicide Prevention Lifeline at 1-800-273-8255. They are a nationwide toll-free service that will assist the caller to get in contact with the local suicide prevention and mental health service provider. The NSPL is made up of over 150 crisis centers across the United States and is staffed with professional crisis support. These people are the real deal and they've assisted in the preservation of many lives.

Play Ball!

Many smaller incidents through my middle school years blended together- especially with the frequency and, admittedly, the consistency and monotony of the abuse. Everything seemed to have a cadence, tempo, or script. It got to the point where I could tell simply by looking at Leader or a select few of the followers if I was going to have a bad day. However, one incident specifically has left an indelible mark on me.

In the spring of 1997, still my 7th grade year, I was excited. First, school was almost over. Second, and more importantly, baseball was starting up and tryouts for the school team were quickly approaching. The gym class was coming back into the school after playing Wiffle ball outside. I was the last one in because I was talking to Coach about tryouts and helping him clean up. Despite my feelings toward Coach, I still loved baseball and wanted to play every chance I had. This included playing for the school team under Coach's direction and calling some of the followers teammates, if only for a few short weeks.

As I walked ahead of Coach into the building someone caught my attention from the lower landing by calling out, "Hey Andy." As I turned to my right to look where the voice was coming from I was hit just behind my left temple by a rubberized softball, the same ones I mentioned before. Then someone behind me hit me square across the shoulder blades with a Wiffle ball bat filled a third of the way with sand and gravel. I staggered down a flight of stairs while covering up my face and head as best as I could as my aggressors raced down the stairs and into the locker room laughing. I stayed in the corner of that stairwell for a few minutes as I regained my orientation and my breathing.

We weren't playing Wiffle ball with a "corked" bat or the rubberized softballs so it's evident that this attack was planned and orchestrated. I don't know what it was about me that made me such a desirable repeat target. Perhaps they knew the gang mentality was an effective means to get a cheap thrill. They knew they would get quite a show with little to no resistance due to the immense show of force with a "loaded" bat and rubberized baseballs thrown at full speed. At this point my reflexes were getting better at catching and dodging the ties, belts, and shoes. Even when they connected I was so acclimated to the feeling that I stopped responding with pain and started to defend myself. Maybe they needed to up the ante in order to shift the fight further in their favor.

Last Stand

The last major incident happened in eighth grade. At some point everyone has their Breaking Point- that point where the frustration and anger of the situation surpasses the fears and risks that have stood in the way for so long and action must be taken. The scene was much the same- the boys' locker room after gym class. The verbal sparring was starting to get testy and some of the boys started snapping their belts by holding the end and buckle in one hand, placing their thumb in the crease, and quickly pulling it apart creating a sharp crack. As I turned to grab my shirt I felt the familiar stinging of a tie being raked across my back. I turned around in time to catch the next one but two more kids were already joining the melee. The problem with boys as they grow older is that they become bigger and stronger. Some of them were now bigger, faster, and stronger than me which made the ambush even more difficult. I had had enough of their abuse. I was too old, too tired, and too frustrated to let this happen anymore. I knew I couldn't beat them so I did the next best thing; I grabbed all of my clothes and I ran. I ran out of the locker room and took a sharp left turn down the hall that led to the cafeteria. I could hear them as I raced out of the room.

Half of the kids laughed and jeered. The other half panicked, knowing full well that a teacher would eventually be informed of the situation. I burst through the back door of the cafeteria without many clothes on, only to find it full of kids. Instantly, every pair of eyes- girl, boy, adult, and child- was suddenly shifted to my location. Their looks of being startled turned into looks of wonder, concern, confusion, and shock. Holding my clothes in front of me to hide my extensive degree of undress, I quickly jumped behind the serving counter of the cafeteria and ran into the music room. I ducked behind my drum set (which was there because the school didn't have any proper percussion equipment for our newly formed concert band) and started to change hurriedly because I knew that I caught the eyes of a few teachers. One of my confidants- my homeroom teacher- rushed into the room and, with exasperation, asked what was going on. I informed them what happened and they immediately took off to the boys' locker room. I quickly put my shoes on and caught up to them as they entered the door to the hallway leading to the locker room. Not wanting to appear to be a snitch or a rat I passed the teacher yelling that we're coming in- only to be met with a shoe zipping by my head which I ducked, resulting in it flying into the hallway, almost hitting the teacher. The teacher burst into the locker room and asked frantically who threw the shoe. Everyone stood in dumbfounded silence and their various stages of undress as the teacher berated them for their actions and interrupting their class to speak with them. Drastic times evidently required drastic measures.

Eighth Grade Ally

Earlier, I mentioned that when we're going through a difficult stage that we should stay on the lookout for helpers. The memory of one such person came to me late in the brainstorming phase of this book. I had honestly forgotten what a huge positive impact they had made on my life in middle school. They were certainly my ally in eighth grade. Looking back, I tried so hard to be cool and to fit in... and I failed so miserably at both. This teacher was an integral and crucial contributor in helping me to keep what little sanity I had left at that point. They were so intuitive with observing the body language and speech patterns of the students that they were able to connect on a far deeper level with us. They were able to recognize when I was feeling "off" just by watching how I carried myself or how I spoke. They knew I was capable of handling the class material and they allowed me to write as much as I desired without question, without judgment, and without interruption. On days that I was particularly off my baseline, which was evident enough that they readily recognized and acknowledged it, they would "check in" with me with a simple look from her desk while everyone was working on their class work. If I nodded, they knew I wanted to "check out" to the office where there was less sensory and environmental stimulation.

Outside of being overly perceptive and attentive to my behavior, I believe the reason why we connected so well was because they were prone to being talked about in a negative way by students because of their appearance. I can't confirm this, but I wonder to this day if they projected what they wished they was able to do when life got a little too real for them. Looking back, middle school students were ruthless. We, yes myself included -occasionally, admittedly- were equal opportunity antagonists. I remember having nicknames for all of my teachers- regardless how I felt about them- that identified and amplified their worst attributes.

Middle School Wrap Up

To say that middle school was the most trying time in my life would be a gross understatement. Despite working as a federal agent and a correction officer, I have never been in as many life threatening situations as I was in middle school. The scary part, upon reflection, is that the threat was internal. *That* is an important distinction- the stimuli, the *triggers* for the reactions, anxiety, and depression were external. The source, the root of my aggression, low self esteem, and negative self perception was my lack of mastery of myself. I don't blame anyone because I didn't have the necessary tools built up in myself to negotiate a volatile and ever-evolving situation like middle school. That's the purpose of this book- to stress the importance of teaching these skills to *everyone* because I strongly believe that, if everyone masters the ability to help themselves, and help one another, then we'll all be much better off.

The Sad Truth About Leader

(Note: I struggled to find a spot for this chapter. It doesn't belong in any of the upcoming sections and it didn't fit well "in the moment" when going into detail about the abuse. However, I feel that Leader deserves to have his story shared so that others may learn and benefit.)

As time has gone on, I have discovered that there is more to Leader than what was presented to me (and thus, you) to this point. Through my own curiosity, I discovered that I have worked with Leader's father. Once I made the connection between father and son, I asked how Leader was. His father said he was having a very rough go of it. I would be lying if I didn't admit that I initially felt a bit of redemption in a sense that karma had found its way around to complete the circle. I envisioned him dealing with a touch of the flu, perhaps, at most, unemployed and having money issues. Sadly, (and I mean that sincerely) that was not the case. Leader's father detailed a long history of battling mental health challenges. Leader had multiple suicide attempts on his record up to that point, several severe mental health diagnoses, and had become increasingly difficult to manage which has led to his hospitalization. To my understanding- and I must be clear that this information has not been vetted- Leader is now currently hospitalized for his safety and well-being, as well as that of his family and society.

When I heard this my heart sank. I could never wish that upon anyone, even, especially in this case, my worst enemy. Regardless of what he did to me or put other people through, he didn't deserve to go through that. I felt heavy hearted, selfish, destroyed, and angry at myself for feeling any sort of relief or celebration that he was experiencing difficulty in life.

In retrospect, his current condition doesn't excuse his behavior from years gone by, but I have found it easier to accept his behavior and forgive his actions for myself. I find myself tip-toeing a very fine line between being angry and upset with him for the damage he did and was responsible for while also having empathy and compassion for what he and his family have gone through. If there can be any silver lining to this, it is that, due to his mental health challenges, Leader is in a safe, secure, and humane environment where he can receive the treatment and support he needs and he won't be allowed to abuse, harass, bully, or treat others badly anymore. The silver lining on my side is that I have the opportunity and ability to help others through writing this book.

HIGH SCHOOL
A Place to Call Home

The story had ended the day I graduated from middle school. When I walked across the altar of the local church for our graduation and I received my diploma I felt an immediate sense of relief and a weight lifted off my shoulders. Granted I didn't acclimate to high school as well as I had hoped, I was at least saved from the dreaded gym class. Instead of gym I participated in... marching band. (Yup, huge uptick on the ol' social hierarchy there!) Whatever I lost in the invisible popularity pole rankings, I gained in self confidence, discipline, and being included in a group to which I felt a close connection. Many skills I learned through marching and concert band, such as attention to detail and listening comprehension, would prepare me for future law enforcement training and academies.

I'd be remiss if I didn't pay my respects to my time in the marching band. I felt a sense of importance and direction. I didn't practice "*the drums*" I practiced "*my part*." I was an integral part of something much bigger than myself. That isn't a conceited viewpoint because I firmly believe that *every* piece in a band is an integral part of the music. And it gave me power. In my junior and senior year I played the quad drums-four drums of varying diameter and pitch held in front of me with a harness. There was a particular cheer that we played while in the stands in which I was the only person to play-everyone else *reacted* to me. It was the UMass "Go, Fight, Win"- aptly named because the University of Massachusetts at Amherst marching band used that particular drum-only pattern as their "Go, Fight, Win" cheer that particular year. Did I mention the cheerleaders made a special dance for it, too?! Several cheerleaders would frequently approach me and the band director during the football games to request "the drum song." Picture a boy so timid and shy about approaching girls that he finds attractive having *them* approach *him* so they can dance while he does something he finds pure joy in… Yes, for approximately 30 seconds at a whack, several times per game, I was the happiest boy in a very wide radius. (Somehow I'm tempted to engage in sophomoric humor here, but I'll let your mind fill in the blanks.)

Still today I'll be approached by former high school classmates and I'll only be identifiable as, "The Drummer." Not a bad moniker since I shared the drumline with as many as four other people and there were at least ten other drummers in the school in any given year. Also, as a consummate drum nerd, it's satisfying for me because my favorite drummer, Neil Peart (pronounced "PEERT," like a weird past tense of "to peer" rather than "Pert" like the shampoo brand)- the drummer for Rush- named all of the drum solos he recorded on live performances "The Drummer" in the native language of the location in which the show was recorded; "O Baterista" from the 2003 live concert DVD, *Rush in Rio,* recorded in Rio de Janeiro, Brazil, "Der Trommler" from the 2005 live concert DVD, *R30,* recorded in Frankfurt, Germany, and "De Slagwerker" from the 2008 Snakes and Arrows Live DVD recorded in Rotterdam, Netherlands.

The Letter, Revisited

When I had written a letter I was pleased with, I would hide it in the safest, most secure place I knew no one would most likely go: the shelf that held my trophies (from baseball and bowling- I was an above average 10-pin bowler and, had I known athletic scholarships existed for bowling, I would've probably kept it up and taken the sport more seriously.) and game balls from baseball. That shelf had gathered so much dust and was so difficult to reach, someone would have to have a definite and specific reason to go up there… and no one- outside of me- ever did. My cover was almost blown during my high school years. By now things had quieted down considerably. I was not writing as often, my drum practices were focused more on learning my songs and progressing as a musician than exorcising frustrations and expelling energy, and I didn't need the letter anymore… I forgot the letter even existed. I will happily admit that this time period had shifted my focus to helping others, being very self conscious about changes in my body, being scared out of my mind to talk with girls, and finding the newest, coolest, most obscure progressive metal bands from across the country and around the world. It was not until I was cleaning my room with my parents one summer (I believe it was between Freshman and Sophomore years- so, 1999, if you're a stickler for dates) and I was handing trophies down to my dad to be cleaned off when I stumbled across the envelope. Not knowing what it was initially, I looked at it inquisitively. Unfortunately, my father saw me just as I realized what I was holding in my hand. He asked what I had found and I quickly shoved it in my pocket as I said I didn't know and I'd have to check it out later. Thankfully, that was enough to satisfy his curiosity and the crisis was masterfully averted.

Peer Ministry-
"And It All Crashes Down"

In my sophomore year of high school I became very interested in applying for a special class made up of juniors and seniors that served as a peer support group to others in the school and assisted in facilitating the freshman retreats. I know this comes as a shock that I would apply for a class where we got to help others and share our story so others could benefit and learn. As I told the Chief Experience Officer during my entrance interview for the Center of Coaching Mastery where I received my life coaching instruction and initial certification, I've been coaching my whole life without even knowing it. I applied for and was accepted into the Campus Ministry program.

One assignment that I looked forward to in this class was a witness that we were to write detailing a difficult time in our life and how our faith helped us through this difficult period. This assignment would be used to pick who would help on the freshman retreats and speak during the retreat. As you may imagine, I described in graphic detail the abuse I suffered in middle school, my grandfather's passing, and "coming out the other side alive." Even then, so soon after it happened, I thought that younger kids could benefit from what happened to me. I didn't dare speak about the suicide aspect because I knew the overreaction and the immense unwanted attention that it would bring onto me. After all, this was still before any anti-bullying legislation was passed so bullying and hazing were still commonplace and, for lack of a better distinction, quietly accepted. Also, I think it has a greater impact to hear these stories from ones' peers rather than from a rusty, crusty adult. We had to pick a song that represented how we felt and I picked Metallica's "Bleeding Me" for obvious reasons. The line "This hole in my side is from the tree I planted, ooo it tears me and I bleed," was a literal depiction of what I felt when the abuse was happening and how I felt opening those scars again to write such a revealing piece. As I reflect on this writing process, the song still has an emotional effect on me. Half-inspiring me to rage in celebration and also collapse in a ball of tears remembering where I was and what this song meant to me.

My teacher pulled me aside either before or after class one day to express concern about what I wrote. They emphasized that the allegations I made were very serious and they would have to take them seriously. They asked several times if I was sure that everything in the assignment was factual and if I was OK. The next time we had class, I believe it was the next morning, I was taken out of class to speak with the school's chaplain, a priest whom I have grown to know well and respect greatly. We talked about what I had written in the assignment and he pressed me a little for the names of Leader and the followers. I distinctly remember telling him that it happened a long time ago, a lot has changed since then, and I didn't feel the need or desire to divulge that information. Much like now, it wasn't about revenge or vengeance but sharing information and knowledge. He dismissed me but this wouldn't be the last time I would be pulled out of class.

The last time I would be called out of class would be to speak with the Headmaster. I was called down to the office and instructed to report to the Headmaster's office on the third floor (which ticked me off because I was already on the second floor for class when they called me down to the main office on the first floor- even then I wasn't a fan of cardio). I knocked on the door and I was told to come in. As I entered the office- furnished with jungle green carpeting and a beautiful skyline view of my home town- I saw the Headmaster sitting behind their large, beautiful, wooden executive desk and my mom sitting in a chair with my assignment in her hands. I was asked to take a seat. The Headmaster told me that they had read my report and was greatly disturbed by the allegations that I had made. They asked my mom if she knew that this was going on. Mom replied that she knew some of the stuff had occurred but not to the level I had written about. The Headmaster asked if I was OK numerous times or if I needed to talk with anyone. I reiterated that I was fine and that I wrote about this so that I could help others. They finished by saying that they contacted the middle school and the Principal and Guidance Counselor denied any knowledge of the incident. As I have mentioned, nothing of my reports or claims to anyone were written down or documented in any way, shape, or form. With this in mind, they have a huge case of plausible deniability in their favor. Basically, they could say to me "Prove that we knew this happened," and I would be totally out of luck. I wouldn't have been able to prove my case because I never created a paper trail.

After I got home from school that day, Mom and I had a chance to decompress about a stressful situation and reflect on a rather interesting day. I put my backpack on my chair at the kitchen table, went out onto the front porch to retrieve the mail, and we talked in the front foyer about what led to the report and how she came to hear about everything. When Mom told me that she didn't know the full extent of what was going on I offhandedly replied, "Didn't Vô tell you what happened?" She looked at me puzzled and responded, "No, tell me what?" I relayed that I had used my grandfather as a sounding board for all the bullying, girl troubles, and difficulty making friends. I also shared that I asked him not to tell her anything because I didn't want to cause her any undue stress or make her overreact and make the situation any worse. She then told me that he never once hinted that anything was ever troubling me at school or at home. It became very evident that he, in fact, did keep my secrets under his gentleman's agreement and even took them to the grave with him. When we both realized this we shared a long, hard cry together right there in the front foyer. After that, everything regarding this situation went back into its nice, neat little box for a long, long time.

Mom's Side

One of the main people I spoke to about this project was my Mom. I had the opportunity to ask how things looked during this time period through her eyes. Having that chance to sift through the events of middle school and high school from my mom's perspective and hearing her observations opened up a lot of doors to details, insights, and pieces of the story that I repressed or never knew. For instance, the piece that started the flow of information and an open avenue of communication between us was the meeting in my high school Headmaster's office. Mom received a call from the Headmaster on the morning of the meeting requesting her to visit the school to meet with the Headmaster and the teacher of the Campus Ministry class. She was given my assignment to read and the educators shared that they were concerned of the allegations made in the assignment as well as for my health, safety, and wellbeing. In that meeting she disclosed that she was aware of what happened to some extent but she had no idea that the bullying and abuse were to the degree I described.

Mom's active role in the saga began in the seventh grade after my grandfather had passed away. She became aware of what was going on when she found bruises on my thighs. She only saw those signs of trauma because my boxer shorts rode up too far when I bent down to pick something up coming out of the bathroom while I was on my way to my bedroom to get dressed for school. One of the advantages of being an only child that is male is getting away with periods of semi-streaking in the house. After a brief discussion at the breakfast table she made the decision to get my pediatrician involved. My pediatrician noticed the same bruising during the check up that my mom had seen. After the pediatrician and I talked about the extent of the abuse and the tools the kids were using on me, the doctor conducted an extensive evaluation to check for further bruising and any structural damage. After I got dressed the doctor called my mother in and we talked about everything. The pediatrician suggested that we press charges and possibly sue for damages. We chose not to pursue this avenue. I'll explain that decision process more clearly later.

Mom and I made an appointment to see the Principal after school had ended for the year to talk about what was going on. The Principal was a whole new person in this meeting. They came across as open, welcoming, caring, and concerned. When the Principal questioned why we had waited so long to contact their office I spoke up that it was my fault. I didn't want to draw any undue attention or be seen doing the 'walk of shame'- walking into the school before the school day with my Mom in front of everybody. Mom had acquiesced to my pleading and requests not to embarrass me. Make no mistake, the pleading and requests were flat out kicking and screaming. Also, during that summer between seventh and eighth grade Mom and I talked to my pediatrician about seeking mental health care from a psychiatrist. They believed that some of my challenges were due to my grandfather's death. They cited that my grades had begun to drop slightly after his death in February. This is very true and the drop in grades also correlated with the ramping up of the harassment and bullying. My teachers reported that I was a good student who was well behaved and above average academically, but I would become disconnected in class. My mother described their assessments of me as being almost aloof. I attribute a lot of this to diving into my studies and knowing most of the material before we covered it in class. When I did my homework I would read ahead and teach myself the material for the upcoming class so I *could* check out in class. I spent most of my class time working on my writing in order to check out from the present. I chose not to participate in class because I didn't want to be the "smart kid" anymore. Recounting this difficult time, Mom clarified that there was a six month wait to see the psychiatrist. She stated that she called every week or every other week during the summer to check for any cancellations but there weren't any. My pediatrician reevaluated me before the beginning of my eighth-grade year and they stated that I appeared to have improved. This makes sense considering that if an object is removed from the stimuli then the object won't exhibit the same symptoms. Case in point: if we remove a frying pan from the stove eventually it will cool down enough to the point where it poses no threat to burn anything, nevermind be hot enough to cook a meal.

As it turns out, I've always had difficulty fitting in. Mom volunteered that she has always found me difficult to reach, distant, and even isolated. She told me stories about driving past the elementary school during recess and she'd see me sitting on the curb all alone. I recall being sent to the Principal's office in the first grade for punching a kindergarten boy in the face after he made fun of my haircut and called it "stupid." At the time it was a serious claim but looking back I don't dare say that he may have been entirely correct.

Growing up an only child in a very mature neighborhood (that's a nice way of saying most of my neighbors were retirees), I wasn't used to playing with other kids very often. I was taught to entertain myself (Sadly, though thankfully, "I was taught to play with myself" was caught and struck in the editing phases.) and grew accustomed to creating storylines in which I could facilitate the entire story on my own. Even today, I enjoy time to myself and I keep my close friends in the single digits. I like my quiet life and I'm not too eager to clutter the quiet with too much entertaining any time soon. One observation that was very telling was when my mom shared that I practiced my drums very hard all the time. She assumed (correctly) that I was taking out my frustrations and aggressions. She even went as far as to describe my playing as violent and savage. I believe this was a combination of always playing at my highest energy and loudest volume to expel the demons of the day while still trying to nail down proper technique. I went through drumheads and sticks at an alarming and blistering pace.

What's In a Name?

We never really put much thought into our name. Sure, if we are naming our child it's a huge deal and I've known some parents who should've earned a degree in anthropology for the amount of research they put into naming their child. However, their name is *their* name, not ours. Women traditionally change their last name after marriage but that's the family name, not the primary name.

A name encompasses who we are and is a sorting device in our mind. When a name is mentioned among friends there's a wealth of knowledge immediately conjured in that moment. Height, weight, hair color, facial structure, typical clothing, typical smell, how they stand, how they speak, mannerisms, and everything about that person (including our emotions towards them) are brought to the forefront in a fraction of a second. But what if you want to change that?

When a company wants to revitalize its brand and change the perception of the product they go to great lengths. Logos and slogans are changed and advertisements are rolled out to announce a "new and improved" product. Sometimes they'll even boast that the recipe has changed. We saw this when Kentucky Fried Chicken became simply KFC. Even Apple, Google, and Nike started as different brand names. Sir Elton John was born Mr. Reginald Dwight. Martin and Charlie Sheen were originally surnamed Estevez. Yes, as in Emilio

Estevez's father and brother. Even the greatest, Muhammad Ali, was once Cassius Clay.

Name changes for brands and people alike come along for many reasons. In the fall of 2001 a young Andrew Nystrom wanted to be known in school, at church, at home, and anywhere in between as AJ. The reason was simple: To put the legacy, infamy, history, and reputation of "Andy" to bed for good. Unfortunately, as easy as that is to write and grasp as a concept, it was equally as difficult to employ.

When you grow up in the same neighborhood around the same people, go to school with the same kids and the same teachers for so long, it is difficult to have them address you as a different name. Regardless of the tactics I tried and the measures I took, every single teacher, administrator, and classmate called me Andy. 17 years of conditioning was going to take more than a few weeks of imploring to get people to change.

I recall introducing myself in one class as AJ and all eyes were quizzically turned on me. The teacher fixed her glasses to the end of her nose, peered over them at me, and finally told me that I wasn't AJ. I was Andy and that was the end of the discussion. Other teachers thought it was an attempt at a joke and brushed it off. However, this subject was rooted deep inside me. I drew a hard line in my head who Andy was, what he stood for, and what he was willing to do to back up those stances. Andy was associated with middle school, weakness, being a doormat for others, and not knowing which way was up. I was done with Andy because that name stood for nothing that I wanted to be associated with. In my eyes, Andy was dead.

I wasn't fully able to embrace the identity of AJ until I started my undergraduate studies. I authored all my papers, signed all documents, and introduced myself as AJ without any pushback or argument. Finally, it stuck and I could create some distance between myself and Andy. There are still people that still call me Andy despite my best efforts. I don't hold any negativity or bitterness about it as I once did, though sometimes I choose not to reply as quickly if that name is spoken. My only thought in those moments is the recollection that Muhammad Ali wouldn't acknowledge anyone who called him Cassius Clay and Kareem Abdul-Jabbar would just keep walking if anyone ever called out for Lew Alcindor.

PART III:
THE PROFESSIONAL WORLD

Security & Department of Correction
Part I

Almost directly out of college I started working contract
security at a federal office building in Boston, Massachusetts.
Originally, I worked 12-hour overnight shifts and I spent most
of my time writing and developing a fictional story about-
who would have guessed it- ex-military and law enforcement
personnel teaming up to fight crime when the system- the
politicians and police brass- didn't want to ruffle the feathers
of the local organized crime boss. I worked with my girlfriend
to make plans and figure out what, exactly, I was going to do
with my life. I had plans to go into the Air Force or Coast
Guard to get my veteran's status and get onto a local police
department. (Note: Massachusetts is a Civil Service state in
which police applicants must take a test before being eligible
for hire. Military veterans receive a preference that bumps
them up to the top of the candidate list. Police departments
must exhaust the entire pool of veteran applicants before
interviewing a civilian applicant.) Over time, I moved to a
different federal office building where I was able to get onto
the day shift. It was during this time period that I signed up for
and took as many federal agency entrance exams as I could fit
into my schedule. Finally, I got the call to enter the
Department of Correction Academy in September, 2007.
Before that Academy I broke up with my girlfriend. I cited

nonsense reasons of going through something very difficult, I needed to close ranks, and be alone. I bring this up as a learning experience from the perspective of always being alone when I went through tough situations. It is very, extremely, *immensely* important to learn how to include people in our struggles and our successes. We need a team of supportive people as we go through life. I talk about this more thoroughly in "Developing Our Executive Board." I also discuss the challenges of having undiagnosed anxiety and depression in "My Challenges and Their Value," because this behavior- irrationally questioning relationships and your place in them- is a tell tale sign of anxiety.

After I completed the academy in November, 2007, I was assigned to the more infamous maximum security facility in Massachusetts. The facility had a reputation of being one of the most dangerous and out of control prisons in the country. That reputation became so bad that the citizens of the town petitioned, and won, that the name of the facility be changed as not to reflect the town's name. Even today, though the official name of the prison was changed, it's commonly still referred to simply by the town's name. Furthermore, my introduction to the institution was working Thanksgiving on day shift even though we were on our institutional training week. I was assigned to the super maximum segregation unit where the worst inmates in the Commonwealth were housed. There, I observed veteran correction officers wearing t-shirts that had a hand holding a single edge blade on the back that read, "Welcome to [The Hill], now kill yourself." To quote Cypher from the movie, *The Matrix,* "Buckle your seatbelt, Dorothy, because Kansas… is going bye-bye." I could tell I was going to get an education at this place and I was immediately questioning my sanity and my decision.

Just getting inside the main institution of the prison took its toll. Yes, our bags were checked for contraband and we were patted down and searched to make sure we weren't bringing in anything we weren't supposed to, but that was expected. What I wasn't expecting was the door. The main door that served as the separation between the main institution and no man's land- the official entranceway into the City of Evil with a population of over 700 of the Commonwealth's most dangerous and violent convicted felons- is approximately 4 inches thick and consists of plated steel, rebar, and other fortifications. It was extraordinarily difficult to open. When it shut, everyone in the main institution heard it. The thunderous noise and the wave of concussive energy it put off sent chills down my spine and every hair on my body stood on end the first time it slammed behind me. I was warned about this. While working at a funeral home during my undergraduate studies, I befriended a retired correction officer who worked at the facility I was assigned to. He emphasized one main thing about the door- it takes its toll on everyone. Everybody pays the piper. No one is impervious to it though many think they are. He told me to be careful and to monitor myself. If the door takes too much out of an officer or doesn't take enough, then it's time to get out. That means that if the anxiety we feel causes us to shut down, to redline, on a consistent basis (hey, it happens to everyone, we all have bad days) or if we become totally unaffected and indifferent to the point where it has no effect on us at all, then it may be time to reevaluate our career choice, our assignment, or the facility we work at. In my personal case, my reactions swayed so drastically from day to day that I was cognizant that it was not healthy to have such a dramatic sensitivity or ambivalence to the stimuli.

Every new career is filled with lots of "firsts" but nothing can prepare a person for many of the firsts they witness in prison as a correction officer. Their first inmate fight, their first "officer needs assistance" response, and their first response to a suicide attempt. All of these firsts give a person a whole new perspective of the world. Mental health challenges are prevalent among incarcerated populations. I have witnessed self-injurious behavior that is inventive, impressive (horrific, but impressive), haunting, and sickening.

I have seen an inmate smash a television and start eating the glass and electronics, I have seen inmates light their cell on fire in attempt to asphyxiate themselves with the smoke, I have witnessed the aftermath of an inmate that cut himself so badly he needed transfusions. I have seen inmates smear their feces on themselves and their entire cell as an alleged defense mechanism. This sensory overload leads to desensitization and dehumanization of the staff. I became calloused, numb, and almost immune to anything the inmates could show me.

One thing that became increasingly evident was my desensitization to violence, death, and negativity. Truly, those things are heavily present in the prison culture and environment. A November 2015 report from WCVB TV in Boston[5] reported that 14 correction officers committed suicide across the state from 2010 through 2015. Through my time with the department some officers had become so calloused to this seemingly common occurrence that, upon hearing the news, they simply shrug and ask what job location and days off the officer was scheduled for because their slot was now open. There are some that have let the door take so much that there is nothing left to give. This desensitization to staff deaths should not be confused with gallows humor. This dark comedic art of somehow finding sick humor in tragedy and disgust is something almost necessary as a means of levity and releasing negative energy in such a horrid place. The jokes I heard and the observations that were made bordered on obscene and probably put us on an equal playing field as the permanent residents of the Gray Bar Motel.

An excellent illustration of just how bad things can get and how differently people can react to the situation was an incident that happened shortly after I won an assignment into that same large super max segregation unit right after I had graduated from the academy. An inmate had engaged in self

[5] http://www.wcvb.com/news/alarming-number-of-corrections-officers-driven-to-suicide/36559660

injurious behavior by smuggling a piece of his razor back to his cell and cutting his arm pretty badly. That's an understatement. The walls, desk, bed, and floor of his cell were covered with blood and he was nearly unconscious when the officer found him. Because this happened at shift change we saw the flurry of activity. We saw the officers working to stem the bleeding while the nurse assessed the damage and packaged the inmate for transport. Every single door from the nurse's station to the outside of the unit was being held open by officers to ensure that the paramedics could make the fastest entrance and exit possible, even though it was against normal protocol. And I saw the aftermath first hand. It was so late at night that the investigator had left for the evening. We were told that the cell would not be cleaned until the morning when an investigation could be completed. We finally had the tier (the hallway in front of the cells) cleaned because we had officers slipping on the blood and tracking the biological hazardous material around the unit posing a health and safety issue.

I can't shake the thought of that blood soaked cell, the puddles of blood coagulating on the floor, desk, and bed with a multitude of officers' boot prints tracking down the tier. I had difficulty sleeping for the next three nights. I routinely woke up in cold sweat thinking about that incident. I had a hard time walking down the tier without visualizing all the blood, gore, and human destruction in the cell. Quite simply, it messed me up. Even during my most recent time in that unit I immediately recalled the cell and visual mapping of the carnage over the present view. I know there are people reading this that have seen far worse than I have seen and have had little to no effect on them. I respect you, I commend you, but I am different. Witnessing trauma affects everyone differently. Even those on duty that night had several different reactions. Some people needed assistance immediately after the incident. Still more, like myself, were "OK" (which, as I have detailed, is a very subjective term) but needed mental health care later on.

Immigration & Customs Enforcement (ICE)

In January 2009, I began perhaps my greatest period of growth, self exploration, and self education. I had put in for a transfer out of the maximum security prison where I had spent the first 15 months of my career in corrections. The new facility would be much lower intensity, closer to home, and I could finally get off of the midnight shift. I attended the first two days of my orientation week and all was looking good. That afternoon I received a call that I had been waiting a very long time to receive. Immigration and Customs Enforcement, a federal law enforcement agency that works under the umbrella of the US Department of Homeland Security, was calling to inform me that I was selected to enter their next basic training class. Awesome! Oh, by the way, it starts a week from Monday. Wow! Not so awesome! I needed to give the Department of Correction my two weeks' notice and, more importantly, I had to get my affairs in order. I was given a choice of nine locations throughout the country. I asked the representative where I would be able to work hard and not be in a detention facility (a.k.a. a federal prison). The winner: Austin, Texas.

I notified the superintendent at my new prison in writing of the situation and, after he contacted the commissioner's office, I was allowed to use vacation time, personal time, and compensation time to account for my last two weeks with the Department of Correction. On that Friday, the administration met me on the steps to wish me luck even though I had been in that facility less than a week. That show of support never left me. I don't know if I would have received the same support from the administration of my previous facility. (I'm starting to see a trend of not agreeing with administrations... maybe that's why I'm my own boss, now.)

The next two weeks flew by and before I knew it I was in San Antonio, Texas to sign paperwork and I was promptly whisked away bright and early the next morning to the Federal Law Enforcement Training Center to begin my training. To say that this was a shock to the system in every possible way may be an understatement. I was away from home for the first time ever (aside for two pilgrimages to see two different popes; Toronto, Canada in 2002 to see Pope St. John Paul II and Cologne, Germany in 2005 to see Pope Emeritus Benedict XVI). I was on my *own* for the first time. I had just traveled into the central time zone for the first time ever. And, now I was in hot pursuit of my ultimate goal- to become a federal agent. The next 5 1/2 months I grew academically, emotionally, socially, financially, and any other way possible. I had to grow up quickly and on the fly. I am grateful for my classmates in class 911 (Yeah, little bit of symbolism there!) for their leadership, patience, and understanding. We were truly a team that pulled from the strengths of everyone in order to benefit the whole group. We were certainly more than the sum of our parts and for that I'm eternally grateful.

I was introduced to Austin in the truest Texas fashion. I moved into my apartment (on the third floor, mind you) on June 5, 2009. I remember it, clearly, because it was Day 1 of 60+ straight days of 100+ degree weather. Welcome to Texas, ya damn Yankee!! I didn't know a blessed soul, but help came quickly from out of the woodwork. It was my first day in the New World and I already felt at home.

When I got to work I was welcomed into the small office by a group made up of people from all around the country (and even Puerto Rico). Our small group (less than 20 officers and agents) was like a family. We spent so much time with each other that fights and arguments were inevitable but we had far more laughs and fun times than fisticuffs, and most importantly the work got done despite being understaffed and racking up some of the highest numbers for offices with our mission directive.

So, what does this have to do with mental health and my story? Quite a lot, actually. My two years in Texas served as a large turning point for me. Texas taught me that I could thrive in a positive environment with positive people surrounding me in all facets. That is not to say that my Texas family- the people that took me in and basically adopted me as their son, brother, uncle, and cousin- are better than my biological family. Perhaps the most glaring difference is the socialization and communication at work. The bonds we formed as a close knit group of people were extraordinary and I truly felt like I was part of something bigger than myself. We celebrated birthdays, engagements, graduations, marriages, births, and mourned deaths. As a team we hung out outside of work and spoke nothing about our 9-to-5 (realistically, more like our 7-to-6 but we won't go there).

I'll address this in much more detail later, but make a mental bookmark here- the environment always wins. It's a concept that I had written about before I started going to school for coaching and it's a concept that my schooling really polished for me. It's not new or unique but it's something I hadn't put much thought into before. If you're in a good environment with positive people and positive things happening, you feel good. If you're in a negative environment with negative people and negative things happening, then you're probably going to feel negative. We hear this on the news when a tragic shooting occurs and they're talking about excuses for the shooter- "He's a product of his environment."

Yes, we are all products of our environments because the environment always wins.

The flipside- the internal, self-control side- is that we can alter, leverage, manipulate, and change our environment. Like I said, we'll get more into this later, but our environments are made up of people, places, resources, and actions. Essentially, if all or some of those criteria are moving us away from where we want to go and away from achieving our desired results (I'm trying to be cognizant not to slip into coaching mode just yet) then we need to change that. Texas, specifically the people and the places, were the big environmental upgrades for me. I wouldn't realize this important point or feel it until I returned to Massachusetts.

Department of Correction Part II

I returned to Massachusetts on February 24th, 2011 (the day before my grandmother's 80th birthday) and returned to work in late June, 2011. The tough part about my reentry into corrections was going back inside, the old trauma getting churned up, and witnessing a shift in personnel dynamics. I don't know if this change in personnel attitude was due to a lack of inmates to mess with, boredom, lack of respect for others, or "D: All of the Above" but there was a palpable shift in how staffed talked to one another. If it's known someone is seeking mental health care OR commits suicide, they are considered weak and unable to handle being a correction officer. There was a correction officer that died accidentally due to aspiration after passing out from drinking too much. Some officers were slandering his name and calling him weak for not being able to hold his liquor and not being a "man's man."

After returning to the Department of Correction for approximately nine months I made the decision to apply for and accept one of the open observation tower posts. These are one man posts on the outer perimeter walls where the officer observes the inmate activity inside the walls and looks for any activity out of the norm outside of the prison walls. Officers take these positions for many reasons. Mine was to take a less stressful post out of the limelight and administration's scrutiny while I pursued my graduate education and a change of scenery in my personal and professional life.

One of the more depressing aspects of working in an old prison is the lack of newer technology in some areas. The observation towers were equipped with the old tan or brown office phones with the actual bell and clapper ringer on the inside. One amenity these old reliable phones do not have is caller ID to let the officer know who or what area in the prison the incoming call is coming from. Everyone working on the inside knows this. Something else that everyone knows (and I'll purposely be vague as to not give away any trade secrets) is that the observation towers are armed posts- the officers have access to a loaded, operational firearm at all times. These facts lead into this one: prank phone calls. Prank phone calls can be fun, funny, and entertaining when someone with a quick wit and any semblance of an education calls. My favorite was when one of the new kids who was able to impersonate the famous television sportscaster Howard Cosell called me and "interviewed" me as if I was the boxing "champ" after the big heavyweight boxing match. However the prison brings out the worst in everyone sometimes and we (several of the observation tower officers) received a few calls that simply and succinctly stated "Hey, tower bitch, fucking kill yourself." This is disturbing on several levels. First would be that anyone would say that to someone, ever, nevermind a fellow officer. Second, these comments were made in succession to several towers in a row including calls to people who are not normally assigned on the wall. Third, the statements were said knowing full well that we are armed and that suicide is a huge concern among correction officers in Massachusetts and across the country. Massachusetts is actually second in the country in terms of highest correction officer suicide rate, Nebraska is first. What may be even more alarming is that there's not much we could have done. Because we don't have caller ID, the best we could've done was reported that "someone" called our extension at a specific time, stating what they said, and request the phone records be pulled. I don't know how far the investigation would've been taken, but the other officers and I didn't think that quickly and we never pushed the issue.

I'm not sure what the culture shift has been due to. I don't know where the negativity and cruelty stems from. Perhaps part of it is false bravado, a desire to fit in with the "cool kids," or a little bit too much time on their hands mixed with misdirected attempts at being funny. However, if I've learned anything in my time as a certified life coach and career developer (and I've learned a metric crap ton to be honest- that's more than a standard crap ton, just for clarification) it's that if someone is paying attention to other people's business, they aren't paying enough attention to their own business. The best way I can illustrate this is the idiom, "Those who live in glass houses should not throw rocks." The problem comes when we convince ourselves we live in a brick house (Yep, the Rick James song popped into my head, too.) while standing on the front yard yelling at the neighbors but never turning back to look at our own house to take stock in what's going on in our little corner of the world.

PART IV:
TRAVELING ON THE
HEALING ROAD
(HOW I HELPED MYSELF)

(Note: The title of this chapter is a nod to Mr. Neil Peart's book <u>Ghost Rider: Travels on the Healing Road</u> which details the therapeutic journey he took to exorcise the demons razed by the difficulties and challenges he has faced in his life. As a drummer, intellectual, lyricist, and writer I look up to Neil as a beacon and a mentor. I'll just put it out there that it's on my vision board to meet Mr. Peart. Thank you for your contributions, Professor. -AJN)

The Catalyst

The catalyst for this long, cumbersome, and difficult journey occurred over eight years before I first put pen to paper. In the May 2007 I was working at a local funeral home to supplement my income as an armed security officer in Boston when my partner called me in the early afternoon hours. He is the former correction officer I wrote about when speaking about the door to the facility. He told me that we had to go to Logan International Airport in Boston to meet some human remains that were to be brought back to the funeral home. He hesitated for a second and asked what high school I graduated from. Then he asked the year I graduated. Then he said that he'd try to find someone else. I asked if the remains were of a classmate. He said they were and gave me the name. It was one of my friends who went to the same church as me and we had shared a close moment at the previous Christmas Eve mass. I adamantly told my partner that I would be there. If anyone was going to welcome him back to Massachusetts for the last time it was going to be me.

As I caught up on what happened to my high school friend, I had a tougher and tougher time coming to grips with it. He entered the Navy straight out of high school and was stationed with a Seabees unit in California. After his first deployment to Iraq he got married and had a baby girl.

Unfortunately, the little girl passed away from Sudden Infant Death Syndrome (SIDS) and the emotional trauma was too great to salvage the marriage and my buddy and his wife dissolved their marriage. Shortly thereafter he transferred to a new Seabees unit in Florida and he was almost immediately deployed to Iraq for a second tour of duty. Upon his return he was diagnosed with Post Traumatic Stress Disorder. After his discharge from the Navy, the Veterans' Administration was giving him a hard time with his medications. His dosage was being changed frequently and he would go weeks between refills due to VA paperwork shuffling. The problem with that behavior is that medication needs time and consistent consumption in order to have a consistent result on the patient. My buddy's physiology and mental state were being thrown into figurative knots. My friend was susceptible to many fluctuations between very high highs and extremely low lows that were partially due to a screwed up medication regimen. In May 2007 my friend hanged himself at the age of 22.

I recall going to his wake and funeral with my girlfriend at the time and we wondered openly what had happened and why it happened. He received full military honors and, as they played "Taps" at his gravesite, I wept openly. So many that day thought I cried for him. I did. I was sorry for his family and friends. I was sad my friend had to endure so many hardships in his short life. But truly, I cried for myself. Something in me clicked that day. He could've been me. This could've just as easily been my funeral. In my mind I held the belief that he went where I was too weak to go. Man, he had to be feeling a pain that I had never felt. I have felt a lot of pain and a lot of hurt. To break the ultimate threshold must've been so unbearable and gut wrenching that no person, no mind can comprehend it. It was at this point that I knew I needed to start talking about what happened to me with a professional and seriously consider getting some mental health care.

Opening Up (Pandora's Box)

The first time I told someone the whole story- well, as much of the story that I was ready and willing to tell- was my girlfriend late in college. We went to a restaurant that was our talking spot. We were free to discuss anything and everything there. We had been toying with talking about what happened in middle school for a while- she knew it was something significant and important to me- and I was ready to tell someone. Even being with someone I had strong feelings for and feeling relatively safe, I was still very nervous and had a very difficult time talking about what happened.

When I reached out to her while I was preparing to write this book, she opened my eyes to her observations for the first time. That was my first time opening up about what happened. I still had severe trust issues and she observed that I appeared to just be waiting for her to judge me, to hurt me. She felt that I kept her at an arm's length, emotionally. She was right. Even though this was leaps and bounds ahead of any other relationship I had had up to that point and I felt that I could tell her anything, my own limitations held me back from being totally truthful with her and to myself.

Holding Back

So what held me back? I wanted to seek help for a long time. I started with the Department of Correction in 2007 and I saw some really disturbing things behind the walls. There's a reason they call it the City of Evil. I listened to a lot of the older guys and bought into the mentality that "You're weak if you seek help" and that the thoughts eventually go away. Unfortunately, the thoughts never went away- even the thoughts of middle school- and I started to see a change in my habits and behaviors.

Looking back on journals, I have references of thinking about seeking help going back to the summer of 2007. I was worried what people would think: my friends, family, coworkers. I knew my reputation would be shot at the prison and we couldn't let my ultra conservative Portuguese grandmother know. After all, in her eyes only crazy people need to talk to "head shrinkers."

The Grandmother

I love my maternal grandmother and I feel called to share my family's relationship with her in order to provide a ray of hope- or at least shine a light- on a similar relationship others may have to negotiate in their lives. My grandmother is a first-generation American, born to Portuguese immigrants during the Great Depression. She obtained a 10th grade education before leaving school to work in order to help her family make ends meet- a common tale for people of that era and her heritage. After she had my mother (approximately eight years after leaving school) she became a stay at home mom and never worked a job outside of the house again- again, very common for a traditional Portuguese household. Her job, her life, and her perspective ended at the back door of her house.

After I was born and my parents returned to work, so did my grandmother- she raised me from 7 AM to 4 PM most days. And so began the education process of numbers, letters, prayers, limitations, biases, and chores- i.e. working. I was taught to study hard *to get* good grades *to get* a good job *to get* lots of money *to get* a nice wife and a big house… To get, to get, to get. I was taught to consume, not to produce. Consume knowledge, consume time (work), consume goods, etc.… I was also taught gender roles and family dynamics. My mother was a retail pharmacist and the breadwinner of the family- a doctor of pharmacy who has taught classes in college- yet, she has never been good enough in my grandmother's eyes (and I'm totally projecting here, using the comments, digs, and insults my grandmother has hurled at my mother, as evidence) because she has never been an exceptional housekeeper. The fact that my father was *only* a shop teacher (you'll recall that my grandfather moved through the ranks as a disciplinarian and superintendant, held two master's degrees, and was pursuing his doctorate when he passed away) was almost an insult to the family.

Speaking with many coworkers, friends, clients, acquaintances, and hearing stories shared by others about people like my grandmother in their lives gives me a little solace to know I'm not alone. However, that also means that everyone else- or at least a vast majority of people- has to negotiate the minefield of a delicate relationship like my family and I do with my grandmother. The presence of someone in our lives that sets unrealistic expectations and chastises us when we don't reach them will mess with us mentally if we don't identify where the venom is coming from and neutralize it properly. The negative feedback loop projected onto us by someone that has little to no perspective is dangerous in that we may think it's truly our fault or there's something wrong with us.

First, allow me to reiterate that expectations are based on learned fears, biases, norms, rules, behaviors, and limitations of the person projecting them. When we have taken the time to gain perspective of ourselves through exploration of where *we* learned to fear, judge, limit, project, and expect (et al) we can also gain perspective of others. If you're "grandmother" character (the one you're picturing in your head as you read this) is in your family then you may very well be able to trace the lineage of your own limiting beliefs through them or a directly related family connection. When we (or someone else) speak negatively about ourselves it is ingrained in our thought and speech pattern. Eventually, it works its way into our physiology and we are physically unable to do the action because our thoughts have been conditioned to shut down that circuit! *Shut it down! Whatever the result of that action is will be negative and we need to avoid pain!!* To equate this to cartoons (and who doesn't like a good Looney Tunes reference?! God bless Mel Blanc!), when we let the devil on one shoulder get a hold of a megaphone and drown out the angel on the other side then those negative, nasty, self loathing, self deprecating thoughts take hold as the only thoughts we have, and thus, with no competition, are accepted as fact and incorporated into our daily actions.

The biggest asset that we have at our disposal for these people in our lives is what I call the Independence Mantra- the idea that focusing *only* on facts and no opinions (positive OR negative) can affect our progress. A small example of this was when I had a large, bushy beard for the winter and my grandmother would not stop hounding me to trim it or- best case in her eyes- shave it off. At the same time I had bought some new boots for the winter and had recently gotten down to business altering my nutrition plan and ramping up my workouts. I had lost 10 pounds in three weeks. It was no small feat but even I'll admit that, at that point, it was like throwing a deck chair off the Queen Mary- not many people would notice! My father had noticed some positive changes, so did mom, and even a few coworkers and clients. The grandmother? She complimented my new boots, chastised me about my beard, and sent me on my way. Before, I would've been peeved that she didn't notice my weight loss. However, from my new lens of knowing my self worth, I recognized that she didn't mention my weight- which meant she felt she didn't have anything bad to say. Her silence on the issue in question was the satisfaction I was seeking- though let's be clear, I didn't need it. I am, however, very much human and accolades are often appreciated.

At this point I think it is important (and perhaps requisite) to explain that this section was not to berate or belittle my grandmother. I believe we all have someone like her in our lives and it is important to recognize that we have the capability, responsibility, and accountability to lift ourselves above people coming at us from such a low angle. The combination of effective therapy, rigorous work, and self exploration on my own have assisted me to come to a fresh new level of self-respect, self-worth, and better command over my emotions. Being able to regulate our feelings in a way that embodies the Independence Mantra when dealing with both overzealous critiques AND compliments will serve us well as we pursue our true greatness and our biggest goals.

Holding Back, Continued

Another piece to the puzzle of what held me back was that I was also nervous about seeking therapy. What would it be like? What's wrong with me? Are they going to give me medication? It was a scary prospect to open up about my deepest, darkest thoughts and fears to a stranger. What would they think of me? Would I scare them? What would it mean for my career? Would my mental health challenges cause the department to deem me unfit for duty? Would this jeopardize my career? How would my opportunity to legally carry a personal firearm be affected? I mean, hell, I'm proficient with firearms and I've been trusted around them more often than not in my adult life!

I wanted to get help; I wanted to receive mental health care to help me negotiate and come to grips with what happened in middle school as early as when I was in college planning on pursuing law enforcement as a career. My main sticking point was that I was scared out of my mind. I didn't know what nastiness could be drudged up. In fact, I'm still scared stiff about what else is hidden in my depths but I'm embracing the fear more every day. You see, it's a continual process of self discovery, self knowledge, assessment and improvement. I associate this to learning drums or any instrument. It takes a lifetime to truly master the instrument because there's always something to improve upon. The truth is that we never truly master anything, especially ourselves. It's a perpetual pursuit of knowledge and advancement of the self.

My personal standing with others and how others perceived me used to weigh very heavily on me. What would my friends, my family, coworkers, or potential love interests think of me if they discovered I was seeking mental health care? They would say I'm nuts. "Dude, you're seeing a shrink?! Are you a psycho?! Are you crazy?! Hide all the sharp objects and please stay away from the windows and ledges!" These self projections held me back because I had a hard enough time interacting socially with people, already. I didn't need another reason to slide deeper into my solitary shell.

My biggest fear was the unknown. Just how deep was this rabbit hole? How many more rabbit holes are there? I mean to ease your mind by sharing this next tidbit of information, but I may scare the crap out of you at the same time. There are tons, countless rabbit holes you can venture down. They're like the pores on your face and they're all clogged to different extents; full of oils, contaminants, and other garbage that's in your environment. Some holes are so filled with junk that there like ripe zits and need immediate attention to be popped, drained, cleaned out, and treated to begin the healing process. (The process can be that visceral and gross.) Those are the glaring issues that we *know* about. However, as we know about physical hygiene, mental hygiene works to make our minds a well-oiled machine. When we exfoliate and regularly clean and maintain our mental health, major blemishes are much harder to come by. We'll discuss the comparability of mental, dental, and physical health a little later.

Leveraging My Breaking Point

The first time that I talked about possibly, maybe, perhaps, at some point, kinda, sorta, probably, potentially, seeking the services of a therapist in the future, with someone in the prison (and yes, it was *that* fragile and delicate of a proposition) I confided in a colleague that I respected and with whom I worked well. His reception of what I told him was good. He encouraged me to do what was right for me and to do my homework to find out which therapy style would be the best fit for me. He disclosed that he had been seeing a therapist for years and he felt it was the best move that he made in order to keep his head on straight. He also cautioned that it would greatly behoove me to not tell anyone outside of my inner circle of trusted friends in the prison due to ridicule and uneducated stereotypes amongst other correction officers.

I keep my phone on all night. That practice stems from a suicide of a former correction officer. When I first started at the prison I was on the overnight shift, 11pm to 7am, and we would routinely have full roll calls in the locker room when a major incident happened earlier in the day. One night we were summoned downstairs and we were particularly rowdy. Roll calls were about assaults and other high risk stuff going down inside the walls so guys would often begin to psyche themselves up (regardless how subconsciously this was, that was the root of the hooting and hollering) to go inside the prison. This one was different. The previous night an officer from the 3pm to 11pm shift called all of his coworkers late at night. Either no one answered or they quickly dismissed him because of the hour of the call. That night the officer died by suicide and left a whole lot of people beside themselves because they were called looking for a helping hand and they all ignored him.

We have a custom at our prison where, when someone dies, we take up a collection to assist the family in deferring the cost of the funeral. It has become almost as customary that we all change our Facebook profile picture to the Department's badge with a mourning band across it. Then, that gesture is followed by another gesture aimed at unity-begging and pleading our fellow officers to seek out the help they need and reposting the phone number of the National Suicide Prevention Lifeline (which is 1-800-273-8255 if you need it or wish to keep it on hand). Often, officers will post their cell phone numbers and encourage friends and colleagues to call them when they need to talk and feel no one is there to listen. There are varying messages that reiterate that we would much rather invest our time (one of the two most precious commodities along with energy) talking with anyone that needs a friendly voice rather than throwing a $20 bill into an empty water jug (which, for comparison, is less than one hour's wage for a Correction Officer working for the DOC). There has to be more proactive steps we can take to *prevent* this from happening.

Breaking the Ice

The worst thing that we can do is nothing. That's quickly becoming my favorite sound bite because it is so true. Too many people are frozen in the pursuit of their dreams and goals because of fear of making the wrong move. I'm at a point now where I'm able to help people break through these points of being stuck in their lives. However, not too long ago, I was struggling with the same problem. The resolution of this problem has had a direct correlation to my progression to this point of sharing my story. I had been looking for a therapist for about a year but I never called anyone because I didn't know what I was looking for. Did I feel more comfortable with a man or woman? Did I want more of a psychoanalytical, hypnosis, cognitive behavioral therapy, or Gestalt approach? What the hell do half of those even mean? I knew I wanted help. I knew I *needed* help. I just didn't know where to *get* the help. I had in-service training for the prison in December 2013 and I contemplated speaking with the representative from the Employee Assistance Services Unit (EASU). When I got up the gumption to approach them, they had already left for the day. Over the summer I looked up therapists in the area but did nothing with the information. In the fall I had a coworker look up the EASU number for me and I did nothing with that, too. Finally, in-service training came back around in

December 2014 and I made a commitment to myself that I had to speak to the EASU representative, secure a number for a therapist, and make an appointment. Breaking point manipulated, action plan in place.

I wish there was a more dramatic build up to the magic moment. I walked up to him, let him finish his conversation, and told him I needed help. He asked what I needed help with and I told him I was looking for a therapist. He told me he'd get on it and get back to me before lunch. 20 minutes into the next session he discreetly handed me a business card and said "Call on your lunch break. They are expecting your call."

A few sessions into therapy I knew I made the correct decision. I no longer feared my personal Pandora's Box and everything was starting to come off my chest. I had a better understanding of who I was, what happened to me, who I am now, and how I could better assist others. Let's make no mistake, I am continually progressing. I am always finding and assessing areas of my life to improve upon through the blessing/ curse of self awareness. In order to understand everything that I've been through I had to be brave enough to unlock that nice, neat, little box and expose what I have been holding in the deepest, darkest, and ugliest parts of me to the light so I could examine it and, for all intents and purposes, neutralize it and properly organize it.

To explain therapy in terms of growth, let's associate our personal growth to that of a plant. The root system is how a plant gathers nutrients from the soil and also holds itself in the ground to stop from falling over in the slightest breeze. In order to grow taller and thicker, a plant must expand its root system outward and downward to structurally and nutritionally support the new growth. When the root system reaches the edge of the clay pot the roots either stop growing or they begin to intertwine. This is called being root bound. The roots are bound up and cannot adequately support new growth. In our case, the negativity and the dirty, nasty memories from our past hold our roots in place, impeding any further growth.

However, when we take the time to carefully dig down and remove the structures in the way of the roots we can begin to allow new growth to occur. However, new growth needs to be urged by nourishment like positive relationships, good nutrition, physical fitness, academic challenges, and new, auspicious goals outside of our comfort zone.

Self Awareness Leads to Self Consciousness

After I started therapy, my level of self consciousness was through the roof. I had this perception that, because I started feeling better, having more self awareness, and started regulating and improving myself, that I had some physical marker of being in therapy. My first day back to work I was mentally preparing for a backlash... but nothing happened. It was like the movie Groundhog Day- status quo. There was the usual grab-assery on the front stairs of the prison, I went to my tower, the day went by as usual with the normal cadence of count time, chow, movements, lock in, count time, and I went home.

When you're in a fragile state such as beginning therapy there may not be a whole lot of feelings of empowerment and self confidence present, initially. In my experience, emotions were amplified to some extent and I was vulnerable to the observations and opinions of others. This is not a good combination around a rough and tumble group with the grace and subtlety of an intoxicated rhinoceros like correction officers. We are trained to be calloused, insensitive, and emotionally impenetrable against the inmates, so when someone tries to open up about struggles, challenges, and obstacles, some officers revert back to the immature mindset of "If I don't understand it I must distance myself from it, belittle it, and recruit others to my viewpoint to make myself feel significant and accepted."

It always baffled me how some of my coworkers could be so incredibly dichotomous between their work persona and home life. I know at home they are loving, caring, even sensitive guys however at work they become vial, detestable, and insensitive beings. I know we have to be solid and sometimes cold with the inmates because we have a job to do, but man, we're on the same damn team. We have to look out for one another and take care of our own.

When I shared my experiences of seeking help with a few of my close acquaintances at work, they were all supportive and understanding. Some had questions, others shared that they were in therapy, as well. My openness about my mental health challenges opened up communication among friends. It has also broken down barriers between family members, friends, and clients. One of the greatest tools I have received through therapy has been improved self-awareness. Being aware of my actual self- the components that make up who I am: my talents, values, and habits- has led me to a wellspring of knowledge about myself and others. By becoming cognizant of these components I am better able to evaluate my strengths and weaknesses, compare where I presently am to where I want to be, and leverage and manipulate my environment in order to achieve what I want and pursue the results I desire.

Another difficult part I have had with therapy is knowing that something is there, knowing that the proverbial rabbit hole is deeper, and being fearful and anxious about what kind of dirt, nastiness, and filth exploring the depths of the topic will bring. However, the reality is that when we unearth something ugly and nasty that we hate about ourselves we now have the opportunity- perhaps duty and obligation is more appropriate- to improve ourselves, negotiate, understand, address, and neutralize that part of us that we don't like and replace it with something we *do* like, something we *do* love, something that we seek and admire in others and will assist us in our pursuit of our dreams and goals.

Hidden Signs

I hid many signs of my abuse and bullying. I chose to hide most of the evidence because of embarrassment, being ashamed that I couldn't stick up for myself, and feeling like a failure. I also hid the evidence for fear of retribution or judgment by family, friends, coworkers, and anyone else that might have found out. Many of the signs were hidden by a few simple ideas- creating distance and creating diversions. I spent a lot of time downstairs in my parents' basement practicing the drums. Was this a way of expending energy and releasing aggression in a safe and secure environment? Absolutely! However, it was also an opportunity to avoid talking with my parents. This led to a very full schedule with little time unaccounted for.

With little time unaccounted for came few unplanned interactions. The few interactions I did have with my parents or anyone else I was able to railroad the conversation away from myself. Baseball, drumming, music, sports, school, chores, the weather, and local activities all gave me plenty of conversational ammunition to use. When I was in the throes of severe physical abuse, I would wear long sleeves and jeans to cover up any possible exposure of bruised or broken skin. Thankfully JNCO brand jeans and loose fitting clothing were in style for guys at this point so what was actually a defense mechanism was viewed by my parents and those around me as an attempt to be accepted by my peers.

It's one thing to be aware of what I did to avoid confrontation, conflict, and getting caught. It's another thing to know why I engaged in this behavior and how we can work together to improve our environment and, simultaneously, the environment of those around us. I engaged in this kind of behavior mostly out of embarrassment and not knowing what to do or where to turn. A lot of that was due to the fear of judgment. Our society's working definition of masculinity is entrenched in the idea of strength, emotional security (perhaps emotional obscurity is more appropriate), and an ability to defend oneself. I wasn't proficient in any of those. In fact, we could say that my levels were unsatisfactory after looking at all the data. Despite this glaring self awareness, I wasn't eager to share my awkwardness or embarrassment with my parents or anyone else, really. This was a self preservation move. I'll call it the Adam and Eve technique.

The story of Adam and Eve has it that, after they ate from the Tree of Knowledge of Good and Evil, Adam said, "Oh crap, I'm naked!" Talk about self-awareness! When God came into the Garden of Eden neither Adam nor Eve were anywhere to be found. Adam was behind bushes scared to show God is nakedness (at which point my brain automatically starts playing Ricky Ricardo's famous line, "Lucy, you've got some 'splainin' to do!"). Essentially, when we feel that we have failed those that we love and respect, we cower and shade ourselves from them out of embarrassment. The immediate thought is a puppy hiding in the corner after it drops a hot steamer on the living room carpet.

Dovetailing with that lovely image, if we're being realistic with the pup we probably could've paid more attention to their needs. The puppy is under the assumption that it has screwed up and will be punished. Falling short of expectations is something that is universally understood. Unfortunately, we are taught that avoidance is the best way to lessen the burden or cope with perceived failure or at least failure to live up to expectations.

The three tools that I use to overcome this perception with clients- and I believe are the best tried-and-true methods to truly connect with someone- are a judgment free zone, permission, and self-disclosure. My working definition of judgment is the act of allowing opinions and thoughts to interfere with the communication of others. In order to have a judgment free zone we must have awareness when we judge others. By accepting anything and *everything* the other person gives us as a valuable piece of information, seeing the good in that tidbit of info, and clarifying what everything means to them, we can meet the other person where they are on their journey and help to guide them on their road to progress and success. Think back to my story about my grandfather. He would listen to everything I had to say, repeat it back to me clarifying the main points so he understood exactly what I was saying, then he met me where I was and related what happened to me to something that happened in his life or someone else's life that may assist me. This is almost exactly what the Judgment Free Zone is all about. I have to give full credit to the term Judgment Free Zone to Coachville, LLC- the Center for Coaching Mastery where I received my training as a life coach. I had written about the general idea of meeting people where they are because that is what I needed for myself, but Coachville, especially Thomas Leonard who formed the school and helped organize the International Coach Federation- one of the major organizations for certified life coaches- developed my concept far before I even dreamt of thinking of becoming a coach.

Requesting permission from someone will let the person feel that they are in charge, and they *are* when we're trying to help them. Permission can start with something small such as, "May I sit here?" It's so important to ask for permission because a message is best received through an open door. Even though the person is ready to receive it, if they don't know the information is coming, they may not be ready to receive it and the moment may be lost. There is absolutely no shame and no foul in asking, "May I share something with you?" Or "May I ask you something?"

At this point, I'd like to take a quick moment to beg and plead that we (remember I need the reminder just as much as everyone else) not use any anxiety amplifiers such as "Now, I don't want you to get upset, but…" There have been times that I've walked away from my mother and grandmother when they've said that. My reason? "I don't want to become upset, either!" I feel that an anxiety amplifier like that may be synonymous with saying "Stand here in the ring. I'm going to put on this boxing glove and smash you in the face. Now I don't want you to get hurt, but…" Sufficient to say I call it an anxiety amplifier with just cause. OK, back to your regularly scheduled book!

The last tool is self disclosure. This is a powerful tool because people in a dither, especially younger people, sometimes feel that they are isolated and this is the first time in the history of man that whatever they are going through is happening. But, by using our permission piece- "May I share something with you?"- we can open the door for ourselves to share an intimate story that relates to their current situation in which we or someone close to us has had a similar experience and got through it just fine. After the self disclosure I'll often ask "May I share what worked well for me?" to which the response is usually a resounding, "Yes, *please*" and an inherent investment from the other person into what I'm about to tell them.

These three tools have greatly assisted me in developing deep, long-lasting relationships with people very quickly. Hearing someone out without judging them, meeting them where they are, asking their permission to engage them, and opening ourselves up to vulnerability are great ways to connect with people individually, and combining them only makes them that much more powerful.

Mom's Mistakes

From a strictly learning and teaching perspective we'll turn
our attention to my Mom's actions during my middle school
years. Remember that I was extremely diligent, detailed, and
calculated when it came to hiding signs of the abuse from my
Mom. I absolutely *did not* want her to find out about the abuse
because I didn't want to add any undue stress to her life. Once
the bullying and abuse became evident when she discovered
the bruises on my legs coming out of the shower that fateful
morning she took action quickly. She immediately contacted
my pediatrician and sought his counsel.

If we can garner anything from my Mom's mistakes it is to
stay true to yourself and not to back down, ever. My Mom and
pediatrician did an awesome job of recognizing that I would
probably benefit from therapy. She called one therapist that
she knew and my pediatrician referred her to. When she was
told that it would be a six-month wait she accepted that and,
although she called back every week or two to check the
therapist's scheduled availability, she never called other
therapists. Likewise, when she approached me about seeing
the Principal during school hours I violently rejected this (for
reasons previously mentioned) and she kowtowed to my
requests (demands) as to not upset me too much. A parent's
intuition should not be dissuaded or stifled by a voice on the

other end of the phone or even their own child. If we believe that our child may benefit from therapy then we cannot accept "no" as a valid answer. I implore my clients when they are seeking therapy for themselves to hear "no" as "go"- as in go onto the next person you'll speak to until you hear "yes." Hell, I tell them that when they're pursuing *ANY* goal! My pediatrician also suggested that my parents and I sue the school for lack of action and negligence in addressing the abuse and bullying. That was met with a resounding, "No!" from my parents for a few reasons. The primary factor was we just don't "do that." It was my family's belief (read: perception and opinion) that people that sue are just looking for a quick pay day and don't have the ability or desire to seek a solution or their desired results on their own. The other reason was because we would be suing the church. As a private school run by the diocese, we would be suing the church that we belonged to. In the court of public opinion this would have tarnished my family's reputation and would have cast a dark shadow over our family in the eyes of the congregation. In short, it was a fight we weren't willing to pick.

Putting on my adult pants and looking back on the events, from a legal aspect I don't know if I would have had a case. I could have gone through my journal to see when I talked with my teachers and school administrators but they had plausible deniability because nothing was ever documented by the school. In some way, I do wish we had sued; even if we settled out of court, the discussion would have been started. My hope would be that my actions would have encouraged others that were experiencing similar treatment to speak up and be counted, as well. Alas, hindsight is always 20/20 and we cannot change the past.

PART V:
HELPING OURSELVES
& OTHERS

How Can We Help Others?

Boy, isn't that a loaded question?! I spent a lot of time and energy detailing my story, my struggles, and how I came to help myself. Through my research, discussions, and reflections on my own journey I have compiled some suggestions to help ourselves in our own family, our friends, colleagues, or even total strangers. However, I think the most basic, baseline, generic answer to the big question is to care. When we approach an interaction of any kind with love, compassion, and empathy armed with the goal of respecting the spirit of the other person and celebrating their life, then our presence will truly be a present to them.

One of the easiest ways to detect changes in a person's balance is to observe them. We manage our lives through patterns and rhythms. We have happy patterns, average (baseline) patterns, stressed patterns, and bad patterns. All patterns are as comforting to us as Linus' security blanket. (That's a Peanuts [Charlie Brown] reference for all of you young ones out there.) When our pattern is broken and we're thrown off rhythm, we have to switch our autopilot off, pay attention, and manually steer for a while. That's important. Highlight that line. It's important because that's a leverage point when we notice people are in a bad pattern.

When we are observant of other people and how they talk-
the words, phrases, tone, and tempo they use- we can get a feel
for how they're doing just by checking in. Likewise watching
their body language or even their work patterns can also allow
us to notice changes in their behavior and mental state. When
we notice changes in behavior it is important to be able to
quantify the change and check in with the person as soon as
possible. *(Note: I originally wrote, "When you feel
comfortable" but that's hogwash and I called myself out on it.
Comfort goes out the window when we're helping others. We
will be uncomfortable. It's something I still struggle with, but
we can learn to become comfortable in our discomfort in
order to help one another.)* This means being able to identify
and quantify a person's baseline behavior and then citing the
specific changes in their current behavior that raised a flag for
us. A good example of this occurred in the Fall just after
football season started. In my close knit group of 4 to 5 guys
at work we usually tell each other when we're taking time off
and someone will text or call someone if they aren't feeling
well and they're calling out sick. One of the guys in the crew
did not show up for work three straight Sundays in a row.
Through a lot of talks and opening up he disclosed over time
that he is also challenged by PTSD and likes his occasional
alcohol. He had struggled monitoring his alcohol intake to the
point where he had made some reckless decisions. The
weather was starting to shift and I was feeling a little
depressed so I assumed he could be feeling some of the same
effects. *(Note: This was before I got serious about my self care
regimen and I had not yet started to take St. John's Wort. St.
John's Wort is a medicinal herb that has properties that can
assist with lessening symptoms of depression. Speaking as
someone challenged with low level depression, general
anxiety disorder and Post Traumatic Stress Disorder, I
experienced excellent results from maintaining a St. John's
Wort regiment. I felt positive effects within the first day. This
regiment, partnered with a good nutrition plan, solid workout*

regimen, and a self care regimen that includes meditation, yoga, journaling, and minimal aromatherapy, has helped me to dramatically improve my quality of life. Also, this is an awesome example of projection on my part! "I am feeling this way therefore he must be, too." I have to own that and work on it.) I spoke with a few of the other guys and he hadn't told anyone about taking any time off. I checked in with him via text message. I pointed out that this was the third Sunday in a row that he was out of work without telling anyone and I asked if everything was OK. He responded that he had some "use or lose "time to burn so he decided to extend his weekends for a couple weeks. He recognized that I addressed the issue head-on, right away, and he appreciated it. He realized I noticed a change in his pattern and thanked me for looking out.

For every positive story there is a flipside and not everyone will be receptive to our efforts to assist them. Another coworker was in a bad pattern of negative self-talk, catastrophizing recent events, and having an overall gloomy attitude. When I asked what he wanted in life he responded that he wanted to be a police officer. Awesome! We have a direction and a desired result! I conducted my usual curious and creative exploration of his environment. When we started to explore his possibilities for finding employment opportunities he began to withdraw. He said he wasn't a veteran and he had no shot in Massachusetts because he didn't score well on the civil service test. The next day I gave him links to police departments in others New England states that were hiring, were not civil service departments, and were looking for candidates with his specific skill sets. At that point he totally retracted, said that wasn't an option, and said he had to deal with his challenges on his own.

At times like this we often question our abilities and motives. We can't let it dissuade our efforts because helping people is in our nature. Many times, people have a lot of sticking points in their various environments that do not allow them to pin back their ears in one specific environment. For example, I know that this coworker has a very close connection with his family. His valuation of the closeness he shares with his family is greater than his valuation of the job of his dreams. This illustrates the very important point that I forgot in this case: the only way to influence and assist someone is to learn what or who they are anchored in and use that to our and their advantage. By learning a person's values, morals, and absolutes (meaning what constitutes totally 100% yes, and total 100% no) we can tailor our message and approach to their unique personality.

The Skeletons in Our Closets

The idiom "skeletons in our closet" is a scary and dicey topic to broach- but so was opening this book in such a brutally honest fashion. I firmly believe that everyone has skeletons in their closet. We know they are there but we don't want to deal with the pain, discomfort, and nausea of addressing the past. I think the disconnection comes from a mindset that "If I just ignore them, they'll go away." This couldn't be farther from the truth. The two biggest things running through my head are "Know thy enemy," and "The best defense is a good offense." In order to handle our skeleton situation in the most efficient and effective way possible we must identify the skeletons individually. They are what, specifically, is blocking us from accessing our true greatness, our gifts, and impeding our progress to pursue our desired results. I believe skeletons fall into two categories- transgressions and omissions.

Transgressions are things that we did or happened to us that we have held onto as symbolic tokens of negativity. These provide false evidence that we are not good enough, people suck, or other similar negative thoughts. Omissions are things that we did not do or things that were not done for us. These are very real examples that fear is a major factor. Omissions are most likely due to fear. As I'm writing this I'm flashing back to four specific young ladies I had crushes on in high school that have said recently that they wish they went out with me in high school but -surprise surprise- I appeared aloof or disinterested in them! We're going to encounter skeletons from throughout our life- some we have forgotten all about- in various stages of decay. These dirty, smelly, rotting corpses of past transgressions and omissions must be dealt with properly so we can proceed on our journey with a clear mind, clear conscious, and a revitalized spirit. We must work diligently to neutralize their stench, clean off all of the garbage on them, and stack them neatly in the back of the closet so we can use the closet for all our gifts and rewards we'll receive on our journey through life.

Let's get one thing straight and perfectly clear: we cannot remove our skeletons. With that said, the mind is a very expansive and complex organ and, through coaxing, coaching, some creative shifting and maneuvering, we can hide or store our skeletons in a very deep and hard to reach place in our minds. Our skeletons are thoughts and memories from the past. They are the "would've, should've, could've," moments and the "Dammit, I really wish I didn't" moments that act as splinters in our mind and sandpaper on our hearts. We never forget. However, after we have neutralized the memory and reassigned the value associated with the moments we can also make it very hard to remember.

Have you ever gone into someone's house and immediately thought, "Oh, there's definitely a cat in here," because the house reeks of cat odors? We notice the smells because we are new to the environment and the olfactory stimuli is new and in our face. The owner of the home may not smell the cat smells because they live in the environment constantly and they have become acclimated to the environment. Much the same, we become acclimated to our environments and complacent with the skeletons in our closet.

To anyone that cares to enter and pay attention to our environment, it can be quite evident that something is awry and that there are is an unattended skeleton problem present. We knowingly and willingly become addicted to our complacency. In my book, *The Skeleton Key*, I actually go through the seven criterion of substance abuse, because DSM-IV doesn't have a diagnosis for "addiction," and the 12 steps of recovery applying the concepts to complacency. We develop habits, excuses, and entire routines to work around the parameters of our skeletons in order to not kick up any dirt and muddy the waters. This is similar to a single guy (*raises hand) cooking meat the day after trash day (*raises hand). I will do everything in my power to hold onto that meat container until I have enough trash built up towards another trash bag. I have wrapped it in multiple bags, Febreezed the ever living crap out of the container, trash bags, and room, and I've even installed air fresheners strategically inside the lid of the garbage can so when I pop the lid open I got a whiff of evergreen before I smelled the chicken carton. I'll be honest, it smelled like rotten chicken rolled up in a Christmas tree... but I sure as hell wasn't putting out the trash before the trash bag was full. I was going to get my *full* $2 value out of that bag! It's not until we are pushed beyond our breaking point that we take action to address and correct issues like our skeletons. I address how to leverage and manipulate our Breaking Point later on in the book.

When I started game planning for my exit from law enforcement there were a few criteria that I knew I had to meet with my new career: I had to help people more than I was in law enforcement, I had to have more time off for socialization and family time, and, whatever I chose, I knew I had to face my demons and put them to rest once and for all. I knew deep down that I wasn't being honest with myself. The stories I told myself that I was fine, that I was good enough in my current state, and that I was "good to go" were complete and utter garbage, and I knew it. I'm reminded of the movie

The Italian Job when Donald Sutherland's character, John, tells Mark Wahlberg's character, Charlie, that "FINE" stands for "Freaked out, Insecure, Neurotic, and Emotional." At that moment in time I would say that acronym perfectly and accurately nailed my state of mind.

I knew that the better I was, the more I could help others. A lot of changes and challenges had to be made. "A leader will not ask others to do something they haven't or won't do themselves." I had read and written that one line many times but it hit home for me when I reread it in conjunction with thinking of my own shortcomings. How could I ask someone to be honest with me, or themselves, when I wasn't being honest with myself? How could I suggest that a client seek therapy when I hadn't had the bravery, cojoñes, or confidence to face my issues, first? The answer was simple: I couldn't do it with a clear conscience. I wanted to be a leader, a role model, and a mentor. How the hell was I going to lead others when I wouldn't even follow myself?! I definitely wasn't leader material. I knew I had to get real with myself really quickly in order to truly pursue my passions and be able to lead others with a clear conscience and strong heart. Upon honest reflection, I realized that I would see people at their worst. I had to be prepared to face the dirt they kicked up in their life without it kicking up dirt in my own life. I knew that I had stuff I hadn't handled yet and it would do me and my clients a disservice if I didn't square myself away, first. Squared away is another military term that has slipped into my lexicon due to several law enforcement academies and basic trainings. It is a term for absolute organization. When our uniform is pressed crisp, worn well, and boots polished, we appear square away. When our performance is professional and exemplary or our room is in impeccable condition where there is a place for everything and everything is in its place-that's squared away. It's a perfect analogy for unruly, unkempt skeletons impeding our progress.

I had already been going to school for my Master's in Secondary Education but I was unsure if I wanted to pursue education solely as my new career. On Christmas Day, 2014 I was sitting in my parents' house mapping out the major holidays to see how my work schedule landed. Outside of Thanksgiving which always lands on a Thursday, one of my scheduled days off, my next major holiday I would have had off would have been Independence Day (July 4th), 2018! My morale and quality of life was trash and that realization tripped my Breaking Point. I watched YouTube videos of motivational speakers, keynote presentations of business and leadership experts every night after work. I wanted to do THAT; I wanted to help people to improve their lives and assist them in transitioning to their dream job and their dream life. I reached out to people who are where I wanted to be and asked them about the process and a week later I was signed up for classes to become a certified life coach.

Seek Mental Health Care

I suggest to many of my clients that they seek mental health care. Their first question is always, "What?! Do you think I'm nuts?!" To which I assure them that they are perfectly normal. This inevitably leads me into a tangent about what "normal" actually is. At this point I self disclose that I have been in therapy regularly since January 2015 and I believe it's very healthy and acceptable to communicate with a professional about what is going on (or what *has* gone on) in your life. The next question is almost always, "What is it like? Do I have to lie on the couch?" Although some psychiatrists use psychoanalysis treatment in their practice- that's where the "lying down on the couch" thing comes from- most therapists do not employ that specific technique. Our media, society in general, and our culture have sensationalized and exaggerated mental health services and therapy. Most therapy techniques are usually employed by simply sitting down and engaging in a dialogue with the therapist or clinician.

What is Normal?

People throw the term "normal" around way too freely. They toss it about like it has a definite, objective, quantifiable, repetitive nature. These people are sadly mistaken. Normal is actually a shape shifting, subjective term that attempts to describe our acceptable baseline *at this moment*. My definition and my qualifications of normal *right now* probably won't match your definition and qualifications. Hell, my current definitions and qualifications don't match my own from last month or last year and I'll hedge my bets that my current parameters will morph and progress next month, and going forward, as well.

I believe our past predicts the present and our present actions can help to predict the future. What this means is that we can't necessarily help our current definitions and qualifications of normal right now but we can make a commitment and sign a contract with ourselves to expect more from ourselves and to set a new design, a new template of what "normal" *will* mean to us going forward. If we put something in our mind's eye- that is, focus on something several times every day so that it's always in our train of thought- our brains will work overtime to make that vision, those parameters, a reality.

In order to learn how to leverage and manipulate our definition of normal we need to know what makes up "normal." Normal is our current perception of our environments. In order to know where we're going, we're going to need to know where we are. By physically charting out how we currently feel about each of our environments, while citing as many facts and concrete occurrences as possible, we are setting our current state. From there we need to dream big. What is the *ultimate* normal that we want for ourselves? I'll set a dare that was difficult for me to fully understand, at first. The dare is to develop our ideal "normal," then expand that idea by 3x more. So, say from a financial perspective our big goal is to make $150,000 per year. That's a respectable goal that most people can live very comfortably off. Now expand that state of normal to be $450,000 per year. It was hard for me to imagine it at first.

Let's put that number into perspective. Many financial gurus say to spend approximately 35-45% of our monthly pretax income on our house and no more than 20% on our vehicle. With a $450,000 per year income that's $13,125 per month on the mortgage and $7,500 on a car payment. Given that most car deals are six years that's a $540,000 vehicle. Most mortgages are 30 years so that's a $4,725,000 house!

The purpose of the exercise is to get us thinking on a larger scale and becoming comfortable with success. If we're shooting for $450,000, then $150,000 looks like a reasonable goal and it may only be the first rung on the ladder to success. The other part of that equation is to put out the effort to attain the 3X. This is because success takes a crap load more energy (metric, not standard, in case you're wondering) than we anticipate. If we want to lose 50 pounds we're going to bitch, moan, whine, and pout at every turn because it's a stretch for us to accomplish but the goal is totally doable. However, if we adjust our mindset to lose 150 pounds then we don't have time to bitch, moan, whine, or pout because every waking moment and ounce of energy needs to be focused on losing that weight, hitting the gym, staying on our nutrition plan, minding our hydration and our supplements, and staying the hell away from the dessert tray!!

We can manipulate and leverage our sense of "normal" by overshooting our expectations. That's the explanation behind the popular saying "Aim for the moon, even if you miss you'll be among the stars." Shoot for 3X what we truly want. If we get to 3X, awesome. Even if we only get one third of the way, we're where we wanted to be, originally. Then we can set new goals, 3X those bad boys and make another round of significant environmental upgrades!

Seek Mental Health, Continued

One of the hardest, no, *the* hardest part of seeking help was making the commitment. I spent about a year tossing the idea of getting help around and I did a lot of homework. I was searching for the *perfect* therapist. The biggest challenge I found was that there was a problem with every single person I looked at. Either I didn't want to speak with a woman, or the insurance co-pay was too high, or the drive was too long, or I didn't understand the technique they used. I always found an excuse why they weren't perfect. But it was my own fears finding these flaws because I was scared out of my mind to open up and engage *anyone*.

My view now is different. I see therapy as an opportunity to invest in myself. I speak and write often about treating ourselves as a business and a brand. When I started coaching and writing I didn't fully understand this concept but it makes sense. I get more in depth with the topic in *The Skeleton Key* but the general idea is to invest in yourself, "treat yourself the way you wish others to treat you," in order to improve our energy and ability to better serve others and improve the quality of service we provide to the world. We see a primary care physician every 6 to 12 months to check our physical health. We visit the dentist every six months to clean our teeth. We see a chiropractor often for adjustments and the optometrist to correct our vision. However, it is foreign to see a mental health specialist because one must be clinically insane in order to see a therapist? That makes no sense. Conversely, it has been an outstanding experience for me. It has given me much more insight and understanding regarding the reason I thought certain things about myself and the world and, simultaneously, I've worked systematically to improve my mindset and my whole approach to pursue my desired results and living life as I wish.

My first stint with the DOC affected me, as well. Mom reported that I became cold quickly. I lacked compassion and empathy when it came to injuries to other people- inside and outside of work, inmate or coworker. When I was introduced to the prison culture I quickly learned that officers had to develop a short memory, a thick skin, and had to leave their emotions at the door. There was no time for feelings, and emotions could get you and your partner hurt. For example, we had two officers sent to the hospital with significant injuries due to an inmate attack. When I told my mother about it I shrugged it off and told her that the next guys in line had to step up. The prison doesn't stop for injuries and we sure don't cry over spilled inmates. This wasn't me and I hated who I was becoming. We were forced to work overtime more than was agreement upon in our contract, our bodies were breaking down, and our patience was wearing thin. She said I appeared checked out emotionally and that my attitude seemed to resign to the idea that there will always be casualties but the show/ mission must go on. When I asked Mom if anything appeared to bother me she quickly replied with the last name of a notorious inmate. He concocted an escape plan by wooing the overnight nurse into bringing in a bunch of supplies for him. I was assigned to the unit that housed the inmate and the nurse worked alongside us. He was scheduled to attempt to break out on Thanksgiving 2008 but the nurse gave up the plan once he asked her to bring in a gun. He claimed to me that I was number one on his hit list and that I was going to die that night. However, he is a sociopathic manipulator and most likely had similar "number one" stories and enough dirt for everyone that worked in the unit.

Defragging the Super Computer

The idea or concept of the brain working at the capacity of a super computer is overdone. It's true, don't get me wrong... and it's totally overdone. So, naturally, I'm going to refer to the human brain as a supercomputer. Supercomputers act much like a regular computer. They store their software on the hard drive and have many files for many disciplines organized through the hard drive. In a computer, if the files start to get disorganized and the hard drive is inundated with many, many files clogging up the memory, the response time of the machine may suffer and the user may experience some lag time. This also happens with the human computer, our brain. We clog our heads with so much information, and this information tends to get stored in the fastest way possible so we can store more data. In much the same fashion as the computer, our brain, our memory, works slower because our mind is disorganized and we experience a lag in our processing.

We can improve the performance in the organization of our computers by a process called "defragging." When we defragment our computer's hard drive the computer is inoperable. It cannot be used for anything during this process because it prioritizes reorganization over every other command. The files are meticulously grouped by their type and function to make acquiring and processing the file as streamlined as possible. We can perform our own defragging. This can be done through journaling, meditation, game planning, or a combination of all three. I enjoy defragging on a weekly basis where I sit at my kitchen table with my daily planner, journal, master list of goals for the year, and a legal pad. I put on a fresh pot of coffee (the stronger the better), dress as comfortable as possible (usually a beat up pair of sweats, an old hooded sweatshirt, and my slippers), light a scented candle, and put on some classical music (Haydn, Handel, or Rachmaninoff usually do the trick for me). Nothing else is going on- no cell phone, no computer, no outside stimuli- this is my defragging period to set myself up for the upcoming week.

After my defragging exercise I feel focused, energized, calm, and determined to conquer the upcoming week. My goal is to improve every week in every environment. Defragging allows me to assess my goals, my performance, my strengths, my weaknesses, and where I can make significant progress in the upcoming week. The marriage of meditation, reflection, and game planning really works well for me and it has worked well for some of my clients, also.

Always "On"

In law-enforcement, especially corrections, we are always "on." There is no downtime between the walls. Even if we're having our supper in the staff dining room we don't know when an alarm will sound. At least with firefighters they have time to relax at the station, police officers can park their cruiser and observe traffic for a little while, but inside the prison we're surrounded by convicted felons and we know at least *some* of them are armed with makeshift weapons even if they have them just for "personal protection." There's no room for letting our guard down and there's definitely no room for weakness.

A dirty little secret in the law enforcement community is that some members in this line of work see the act of seeking mental health care as a sign of weakness. It is a fairly accepted consensus that "weakness will get you killed." I have to respectfully disagree. I believe having a lack of awareness for our surroundings, having a false sense of bravado or overconfidence, and a lack of empathy for coworkers coupled with an inability or unwillingness to talk about what has happened is what will kill us. As I have mentioned, I operate a little differently than most people now that I have gained a bit of perspective through seeking mental health care as well as helping others. People that believe that seeking therapy is a sign of weakness have probably been taught and learned that exact bias (opinion) from people in their Familial Realm (one of our personal environments compromised of our relationships and interactions with family members*)*, the ones that we tend to trust the most. Remember, even members of my own family strongly believe that only crazy people see psychologists or therapists. In all honesty, it should be as common place as visiting our primary care physician for a checkup or our dentist to clean our teeth.

It is important to know who we are and what we truly stand for from the inside out. As I have mentioned, we are taught and believe so much information that we blindly accept as fact. However, it is truly the opinions and biases of others that have been infused in us so often and for so long that they have become our environment, our role, and that environment becomes as natural to us as the wallpaper that's been in our parents' house for decades. It is also important to remember that wallpaper wears out and needs to be taken down, removed, and replaced with a fresh coat of paint. (In the case of the house that I bought, we had to take down all the outside walls completely to properly insulate the house.) Once we assess our beliefs, biases, opinions, and perceptions of money, faith, jobs, family, friends, our body, health, and our own limitations, we can assess why we are who we are and why we do what we do. Having a reason, mission and vision statements, and a credo marries our heart- our emotional and empathetic side- to our brain- our systematic and intellectual side. Then comes the fun part: we get to decide how we will act and properly convey who we are, what we do, why we are who we are, and why we do what we do. We have full artistic license, freedom, and permission to create ourselves in the image and likeness that properly conveys our mission and vision. This Role, this script that we create for ourselves will be questioned, tested, and ridiculed by people who *just don't get it.*

Opinions have a place in our culture and society that rivals and resembles facts. They are spoken with a sincerity and apparent weight that conveys a feeling of being inarguable or absolute. However, upon closer inspection, we can see cracks in the veneer. Context clues when people start to breakdown their terms begin to appear. Phrases such as "I think" and "I believe" allow us to realize that people are speaking from their own personal biases, fears, jealousy, and limitations. From this position we can confidently hold the line that opinions mean absolutely jack squat. Opinions that others hold of us, those we hold of other people, and even those we hold of ourselves mean absolutely nothing. By acknowledging this we can move forward focusing only on that which can be qualified and quantified as fact.

The last aspect is to treat ourselves well so that we may better serve others. The Golden Rule, "Treat others how you wish to be treated," is very outwardly focused and extrinsic. The energy is going from us to someone else. As we know from our society we can't rely on anyone else to replenish our energy- we have to be self sufficient in that respect. By treating ourselves well- that is, how we wish to be treated- we give ourselves the energy surplus needed to better serve others.

Regulation and self regulation of opinions is very important. Developing the ability to identify opinions from others as they are being spoken, and opinions within ourselves while they are being formulated, is an essential skill needed in order to experience significant progress towards our goals and desired development. I have more filters in place than I can count that I use to evaluate everything coming in and going out for content, quality, perspective, and the presence of opinions. By recognizing and identifying when opinions are present we can either call ourselves out for projecting our views on others or finding the content from others as not being valid due to a lack of factual content.

Creating Our Own Environment

I mentioned at the end of the ICE chapter that we are, in fact, products of our environment. It comes as no surprise that people that come from safe, financially secure, and emotionally uplifting environments generally have less stress and anxiety than those who are brought up in less affluent areas and broken family situations. However, as I alluded to, we have the ability to leverage, alter, and manipulate our environment to make it better for us and work to serve us better. The news is that the environment always wins. The valuation we assign to that news - good or bad- is ours, alone. When we initially inventory our environment we may perceive this as bad news, but if we change our environment we can change our perception. The good news is that we have control over our environment and we can design it as we see fit.

The first step is like Neo from the movie the *The Matrix*. If you haven't seen it, please do. It's a great film that I cite often. This step is to realize that the world as we see it is not as it actually is. We were born in a specific place at a specific time and surrounded by specific people. This is our initial environment. It's a bunch of auditory, visual, olfactory, gustatory, and tactile stimuli that we process and equate with our homeostasis, our "normal." We can decide that this "normal" is not what we want and take measured, prepared, and rational steps to alter, leverage, and manipulate our state of normal.

It is at this point then I'll introduce you to the term SNAFU (SNA as in "snack" and FU as in "tofu") it stands for "Situation Normal All F**ked Up." Yep, it sure sounds bad and when it's used in the military, things aren't looking good. However, as crazy as it sounds, this is *exactly* what we're looking for when we're manipulating our environment. You see, when our homeostasis, our "normal," is thrown out of whack by a change, our body puts out a hormonal warning signal called cortisol that acts as our "Spidey senses" to read small changes. This feeling is the butterflies in our stomach or how we feel when we lean back in the chair too far and catch ourselves before we fall. If we detect something we may trigger the flight or fight response which releases epinephrine, or, as we like to call it, adrenaline. Adrenaline is good because it gives us a short burst of increased speed, strength, focus, and attention to detail. It also lessens the effects of pain and exhaustion. However, when the adrenaline wears off those feelings of pain and exhaustion will certainly be present and accounted for in a big way.

When we are planning and preparing to alter and manipulate our environment we trigger our Spidey senses that we are about to exit our Comfort Zone and about to enter SNAFU mode. SNAFU mode is a term of growth and expanding our Comfort Zone by pursuing changes to our environment that will directly impact the pursuit of our desired results. Essentially, to quote Thomas Jefferson, "If you want something you've never had you must be willing to do something you've never done." In order to change what we don't like about our environment we must be willing to abandon normalcy in that particular area of our environment in order to embrace the opportunity for growth or upgrade at that respective position.

Environmental design is a foreign topic to most people and, when I'm working with clients, it can take some effort over a few sessions to really hone in on what we want to accomplish. Before we start with environmental change, we need to develop a desirable, productive environment that promotes automated and perpetual motion towards our desired results. Think of your desired results professionally, socially, financially, and emotionally. What does success look like for you in those areas of your life? How, specifically, does that mental picture differ from what true reality is presently? Perhaps you see yourself living in a different location, working at a different job, dressing differently, and things of that nature. Document all this information. By identifying where we are now, where we want to be, a timeframe to achieve our goals in, and the quantifiable differences of the two scenarios we can develop a plan to design, manipulate, leverage, alter, and shift our environment to how we want it to be. Remember that this is an evolution, and evolution takes time and persistent pressure.

Small, steady progressions are the most desirable and maintainable in regards to pursuing our desired results. By making small changes on a consistent basis we don't redline, or shock our system and force our body and mind to shut down. Small changes are easier to implement into our schedule: preparing our meals for the week ahead of time, waking up a half hour earlier, or committing to submitting for three new job opportunities every week. These, individually, are tiny adjustments to our mindset and action plan that we can easily acclimate ourselves to despite easing our way out of our Comfort Zone. Conversely, if we attempted to bite off more than we could chew, we can easily become overwhelmed, frustrated, and exhausted. Too often I see clients that are convinced they must take an "all or nothing" approach to obtaining or achieving their desired results.

Unfortunately, part of coaching is allowing untouchable people to try things "their way" before they acknowledge that they may need help. It's similar to a little child insisting they do something "on their own" to assert their independence only to resigning themselves in a huff of frustration that they do, in fact, need assistance. Likewise, all too often we feel that we must do things "on our own" to be truly successful. On the contrary, many- actually *most* successful people- surround themselves with people that are also successful and that will assist them in their endeavors and hold them accountable when they slack off. In order to be successful we have to "ask and assemble"-it's time to develop our crew. It's time to recruit our Executive Board.

Creating an Executive Board

One of the most empowering (and challenging, admittedly) things I like to do with my clients is to help them to develop and assemble their Executive Board. Much like a big business (because we're all individual companies and brands) our Executive Board is made up of people who are where we want to be in various areas of life. We strategically structure our E-Board like this in order to improve our performance in those areas. The development of the E-Board is sometimes difficult because we don't often evaluate the people that are in our lives presently. They are just kind of there. No muss, no fuss, set it and forget it. However, if we assemble a team of high level performers then we'll have to up our game to hang with the big players. By being around successful people (and we define what successful is by what we want to accomplish) we can learn a lot about how they became successful by observing what they do. If we don't understand why they are doing something we can ask and receive an explanation. Then, we can better understand their process of becoming successful in that particular area of life and make the necessary adjustments to our actions or level of output and commitment in order to see similar results in our own lives.

One of the biggest hang-ups that I encountered while establishing my E-Board- and assisting clients to establish their Executive Boards- is humility. The idea that "I don't want to bother them, they're probably really busy," permeates our thought process and we question ourselves about reaching out to them. Just the opposite is most likely true. They have most likely already discovered and established the mentality of 'service of self' and 'service of others' and will be humbled that we recognize this quality about them. They probably reached out to someone much like we're doing now and they're blown away that it's now they're chance, their opportunity to share all the stuff that they have learned from *their* Executive Board members and other important people in their life.

Another big challenge in the development of our E-Board is what I call the slaughter of our heroes. We tend to hold people in our lives on pedestals for no other reasons but longevity and proximity. If our parents, grandparents, siblings, aunts and uncles, cousins, friends, bosses, colleagues, teammates or other people in our environment are *not* where we want to be- living in the house of our absolute dreams, driving the car of our absolute dreams, taking the vacations we want, working the job that we want, living the spiritual or service minded life that we envision- then they are *not* Executive Board material and should not be treated as such. Yes, we can share our big goals with them but, if they don't have a big imagination or at least the big support we'll need to achieve those goals, then we *must* seek our "yes" elsewhere. From the perspective of family dynamics, we do not like the idea of alienating those that are close to us. However, if we allow them to dictate (manipulate, leverage, alter, etc) the design of our environment due to their narrow vision of our goals, then we will end up living in *their* environment rather than creating our own. This is difficult, but sometimes those closest to us don't want to see us fail because they equate "not succeeding" to "failure." We know better, we know that we must try; we will probably experience defeat many times before we experience success but we will gain a lot of knowledge along the way and when that success comes it will be worth the wait.

Social Media &
Distraction Management

Facebook was created in 2004, two years after I graduated from high school. Today, in 2016 when I'm writing this, over 1 billion people are on Facebook and over 100 million people use Instagram. In short, social media is the new norm of communicating and connecting with people… for better or for worse. Personally, I firmly believe that this new medium is for the worse. In 2014 my home town suffered a great loss when a young girl committed suicide after being bullied in what was called the Facebook Purge. *The Purge* is a 2013 science fiction horror film that depicts a world with dramatically reduced crime rates due to a new criminal justice system that allows a 24-hour period where all crimes are legal up to, and including, murder. The Facebook Purge was designed by high school and college students as a 24-hour period to wreak havoc on their social networks. The premise of the attacks would be to "out" homosexuals who had not publicly revealed their sexual orientation, post nude photos of classmates and ex-significant others as a way of shaming, degrading, and bullying these students, and essentially wreaking havoc and creating mayhem in any way, shape, or form possible.

I am very, extremely confident that I would not have the opportunity to share my story if social media was around when I was in middle school or high school. I firmly believe that the misuse and abuse of these forums by school age children is a huge detriment to our society. Most people are now addicted to social media and are obsessed and compelled to check their profiles and the profiles of others constantly. Aside from abusing time- one of the most valuable commodities in the world (the other is energy)- it also shows an addiction to complacency and an insatiable attraction to external validation and extrinsic affirmation. Everything is posted to grab attention, obtain validation, and receive affirmation from a network of people- most of whom we haven't seen in person in weeks, months, or hell, possibly EVER.

My approach to social media has changed dramatically since I adopted the model of treating myself as a business. The concept of treating oneself as a business is nothing new, but I hope that the trend grows because I am totally invested to it and it has paid unspeakable dividends for me. The principle is simple when applied to social media and everything else in life: if an action does not promote personal growth, progress towards my desired results, or gets me closer to achieving my goals then I do not engage in it. That's important, highlight that. I do not compare myself to other people because it is useless. We are all different, working with different skills, pursuing different goals, and are in different stages of different pursuits. It is illogical and a complete waste of time to engage in frivolities on social media. If we're paying attention to other people's lives, then we're not paying attention to our own life. There's way too much work to be done in every facet of our lives for us to be dedicating hours of our time gawking at what other people are up to.

We are products of our environment *and* we have the ability to design, leverage, manipulate, and change our environment. I know we all want love. I get it. Acceptance, popularity, likes, shares, comments- they are all love on a sliding scale continuum. One of the most liberating experiences of my life was when I voluntarily left social media for 35 straight days. Five straight weeks of no Facebook, Twitter, Instagram, Snapchat, and YouTube allowed me to realize how much time I was wasting and how distracted I really was. To change the behavior we must replace it with other, positive behaviors. I switched social media with my daily planner. I swapped in books and writing (even some sections of *this* book) with Facebook and Instagram. I replaced YouTube and Snapchat with working out, improving my nutrition, and researching more for my clients. Oh, and when I got back to social media I planned my posts ahead of time- even scheduling them so I didn't have to physically be on the computer or my cell phone at a specific time, and I became a producer rather than an observer. What's the difference between a producer, a fauxducer, and an observer? The answer is focus- where the time and energy is spent. And observer is someone that looks, likes, and comments on other people's posts, pictures, and shared articles. Their focus is on consumption. They consume anything and everything- and they want everyone to know it. If we find ourselves 30 pictures deep in a buddy's vacation photo album and we're clicking through like it's our job- we're observing... and wasting time.

The fauxducer is someone that believes and says they're producing but they aren't producing on a daily basis, multiple times a day, and they're observing way too much. Their focus is on image and perception. If they are perceived by others to be a producer, then that's good enough for them. Finally, a producer is someone that's turning out content multiple times a day (scheduled over several platforms) and focused on the next achievement. They treat social media as a tool to reach an extended network. They respond to every comment and have a healthy relationship with their audience without committing too much time away from their product.

How can we improve our communication?
Communication is driven by intimacy. Intimacy is knowing
that an inflection in your buddy's voice means he's playing but
there's half a truth there, as well. Intimacy is calling the client
when a text or email doesn't look great and a few minutes on
the phone will save a lot of time and energy in clarifying and
rectifying terms through written words. Intimacy is meeting
with a friend to talk about their trip rather than being the
Facebook stalking observer example earlier.

Because the value (investment of time and energy) of
intimacy is so high we must be cognizant, cautious, and
creative with the placement and timing of our investments.
Dude, English, por favor?! Basically, don't waste time in
places where, or with people with whom your investment isn't
appreciated and/ or (this is very important) yields a high return
on investment. They have to be equally invested in order for
the relationship to produce respectable dividends. For
example, in *The Skeleton Key,* I wrote about reaching out to a
young lady I have liked since high school but I never had the
Moxie to ask her out. She and I have been friends on social
media for a while and we kept in touch, periodically. Finally, I
reached out to her and I was shutdown. This illustrated a few
points. The first was I was totally an observer in her life: I
hadn't seen her in years, I randomly popped back on the radar,
and I wasn't a physical presence in her life. The other was that
I was looking to invest in someone that had no reason to invest
in me. Now, had we reconnected at a party and hit it off, then
we would've had that initial intimate investment and we
could've used social media as a supplemental investment.

This leads me to my next point. Stay in the present day.
Don't go chasing the past. Those people didn't make it to our
present for a reason. Now, if those people reappear in present
day and there's something there, then that's different. For the
most part it's safe to assume that the people in the past were
meant to stay there. Also, learn to move quickly and
decisively. Steve Harvey wrote in his book *Act Like a Success,*

Think Like a Success that we can't tell our big goals to people with small imaginations. If we have a big goal or an awesome dream that we're pursuing and someone doesn't get it, doesn't believe in us, or simply "can't see the forest through the trees," then we need to thank them for their time, excuse ourselves, and find someone else to talk with. This is exactly what I wrote about at the end of *Designing Our Executive Board*. Likewise, if we're looking to invest in someone (either business or personal) and they're not looking to invest in us, then we need to pick up and move on.

From a guy's perspective- since it's the one I know best- if we're interested in a young woman and we approach with openness, vulnerability, and honesty but she is playing games then it's best to thank her for her time and show ourselves the door (at least be a gentleman and pick up the tab, as well). Either we called it right and she's not ready for an investment or we pushed her hand and created a great leveraging tool- exclusivity and scarcity.

Ladies, you have the same power. If you're interested in a man and he's on the fence simply hold your ground, thank him, and move on. If he was testing the waters but he was initially interested then he has some quick math to do. If you're worth his investment then he's going to have to increase his time and effort to earn your investment after you've walked away OR he'll decide that you weren't worth the investment. NOW, the important part of the equation, if the other person isn't ready for an investment then they aren't worthy of your investment. Let's put it another way: if they're not willing to invest their time and energy into the relationship and they did not see value in us then there's no reason in hell we're going to invest our hard earned time and energy on them. If someone does not see value in us, then the value we see in them isn't worth our investment. I saw a great meme before I got off social media that drives this point home, "Those who doubt me today will be the ones asking how I did it tomorrow."

Permission Complex

One way that we can help everyone, including ourselves, is to listen to understand. Of course, the first part of the equation is to understand ourselves. That's what the rest of this book is for. Most people listen to respond. In our "go, go, go" society we often feel compelled to keep the conversation moving. Moreover, whatever we are hurrying the conversation to get to is often something that will not progress our personal game any faster. Listening truly is an art. In fact, if we so desired we could spend a great deal of time learning the finer points of listening and interpersonal communication. Listening, and talking, is a whole body interaction. We use our breathing, tone, tempo, voice fluctuations, facial expressions, hand movements, body shifts, and many other subconscious non-verbal cues to convey our full message. Truthfully, we convey much more than we wish to. However, most people do not focus on too much past the verbal cues and the more obvious physical cues.

    One tool that I use in coaching (and honestly, everyday life) is called Triplex Listening. As one could probably deduce by seeing the prefix "tri," it has three components: what people say, how they say it, and what they don't say. Observing what people say is the easy part. We listen to their words and filter them for accuracy, context, and meaning.

Observing how people say things is a perpetual endeavor. We could study every word ever spoken or written and question why statements were worded a certain way or why people moved a certain way when speaking about something difficult. My favorite example is something I observed while coaching a client. They would bring up their mother quite often in our calls and I routinely noticed a pause after they said "Mom". One day, when my client was in a particularly spunky and energized mood, I called them on this observation and I asked if we could explore that pattern in their language a little deeper. The mood, tone, and feel of the conversation changed *totally*. The cold, dark feeling of that pause now infiltrated the whole conversation. That small observation unearthed a whole treasure trove of emotions, challenges, goals, and obstacles stemming from their mother and her projected biases, opinions, expectations, and prejudices. There was a whole world waiting to be explored in a short, little, seemingly meaningless pause. This is why texting and social media are so difficult for gauging sincerity. It takes more of an investment, but speaking on the phone or posting a video means so much more because of the inherent clarity of the delivery. I hate wasting time in a 30 minute text conversation or an email chain clarifying and explaining what I meant when a five minute phone conversation will explain everything. Make the investment up front and make better use of your time.

In much the same fashion, Triplex Observation is observing what people do, how they do it, and what they don't do. This practice can help determine the difference between a producer and fauxducer in real life. Many people cast the persona of being productive however it's usually a guise from really just being busy. Being busy is a modern euphemism for doing a lot of menial tasks that take up a lot of time but lead to very little progress. Many fauxducers will talk a good game and make sure many people will know how much work they're doing and may post often about having "So much work to do," or "No time to breathe," or "Always hustling." I will not claim to be hustling like mad, but I can say with 100% certainty that, in order to have enough time to post a meaningless status on social media drawing attention to how much work a person has to do, then they definitely *do* have enough time to breathe and they're definitely *not* hustling hard enough.

Another tool that provides a lot of leverage in the listening game is clarification. Keeping with the theme of understanding others and knowing where they are coming from, clarifying their terms and statements not only puts them in charge of the conversation but allows them to share how they interpret their perspective and how things fit together in their world. This not only earns points with the speaker for our invested interest but allows us to gain intimate insights into the speaker's personal situation. The famous Led Zeppelin song "The Stairway to Heaven," contains the lyrics, "There's a sign on the wall/ But she wants to be sure/ 'Cause you know sometimes words have two meanings." Words often have more than two meanings and can have many more ways of impacting a person. Clarifying what weight a word carries for a person allows us to take a peek into their world and poke around a little bit. Asking "What do you mean by that?" or "Could you explain what that means to you?" from a truly invested, genuine, empathetic position will open up and deepen our relationship with that person.

Think for a moment. If you're on a first date, meeting with a prospective supplier or partner for your business and they start asking questions to know exactly what you're looking for, where you stand, why you feel that way, and how they can assist you to get where you want to go, you're probably going to react pretty positively. "Holy crap! This person cares about me and wants to know me on a deeper level. They "get" where I want to go and they asked me to clarify my plans regarding how I think I can get there." Deepening our relationships with family, friends, coworkers, and clients as well as endearing ourselves to perfect strangers by truly caring and clarifying what they mean will provide us with instant credibility and the proverbial keys to the castle when it comes to earning the trust of others.

Weight of Our Words

One thing we don't always consider is the weight of our words. The manner in which we choose to identify and communicate with others is so important not only for presenting and representing ourselves in a manner that is in line with how we wish to be perceived but also preserving the respect and dignity of our conversation partner while lifting up their confidence and personal standing. So, what that means in plain English is: by constructing and employing our lexicon, our vocabulary, in a way that respects and raises us to the level we wish to portray ourselves, we in turn, respect and raise up the people with whom we are speaking, as well.

The secret to this (and I stress that "the secret is, there is no secret") is striking a careful balance of speaking *to* the people rather than using language and structure that speaks down to, or condescends, our audience or neglecting our intellect, dumbing down the conversation, and pandering to the person. One of my gifts is that I can strike up a conversation with anyone between the ages of 5 and 95 and make a significant connection. To be honest that range is probably a bit broader. I do this by following a few basic cues I have gathered through my life.

The first cue I actually stole from the Disney cast school of communications; meet people on their level. If the person is seated in a chair or even on a step I make it a point to sit, as well, or get down to a comparable level. Likewise, I have no qualms or hesitations getting on one knee to talk face to face with a child. If a person approaches my table, I will either welcome them to an open chair or stand to converse with them away from the table. We are all equals in this world and we can (and should) learn something from every conversation. The faster we learn and apply this, the richer and wiser we will become.

The second cue is to find common ground. I believe that there are degrees of this art, as well. Basic talking points include family, history, arts, and the surroundings on a surface level. I may ask the 5 year old about any siblings or pets they may have whereas I may ask the 95 year old if they come from a particularly large family or an immigrant family. As a former Immigration Enforcement Agent, I am fascinated by stories of migration to this country. The next level requires a more in-depth command of various age groups and demographics. It takes a certain amount of commitment and desire to be able to have an educated and heartfelt discussion about Sesame Street with a 5-year-old (The puppeteer that portrays Big Bird is originally from Massachusetts. Thank you, Mr. Carroll Spinney!) and turn around to have an equally well educated discussion about jazz and big band musicians with the 95-year-old. (My drum instructor originally took lessons from Bill Flanagan who played in Tommy Dorsey's band- Mr. Flanagan also taught Steve Smith, the former drummer of Journey.) This "Jack of all Trades" approach takes time and skill to collect tidbits of knowledge about sports, music, entertainment, and politics from various eras.

My last cue, unfortunately, I cannot teach. However, I believe everyone has it, but some may need to work diligently to uncover and develop it. "It" in this case, is true, unfettered, unbridled empathy, curiosity, and creativity. My empathy, my ability to understand and share feelings with other people, is my bread and butter in business and in life. When we are able to genuinely connect with someone on an emotional level AND tap into our professional skills and abilities to serve them and improve their quality of life, then we will truly know success and happiness will truly seek us out.

Jon Taffer, the host of the television show Bar Rescue and author of *Raise the Bar*, says that everyone sells reactions. Musicians sell reactions in the form of their music and live shows and the feelings they conjure up. Bars sell reactions by how we feel in the atmosphere of the lounge. Everyone everywhere is selling reactions. Mr. Taffer's viewpoint is very external and extrinsic. If I apply Mr. Taffer's approach from an empathetic angle (not very much Taffer's style, admittedly) I would say that everyone everywhere *serves* others. The main way we serve others is through actions- we don't converse much with our garbage collectors (hell, I don't even get to see mine) but they serve us and I am eternally indebted to their services. Actions certainly do speak louder than words, but words often mean more to us. If we aren't invited to a party, then that might suck that it was an oversight. It would suck ten times worse if the host approached us individually and said, "You're not invited to my party." Even in that moment that person is selling reactions (to us and anyone in earshot) and serving us (albeit in a negative manner).

Our words certainly do carry a weight to them. Two ways to honor this is to say things as nicely and personably as possible while citing facts and defusing negative situations as quickly and quietly as possible. Let's handle that second part, first. The easiest and cleanest way to diffuse an argument is to cut losses and create distance. I have found that the most disarming phrase in the English language may very well be, "You're right, I'm sorry." In one felled swoop we are acknowledging fault and apologizing- certainly not a tactic expected in a tense situation. Subconsciously, this is saying, "This isn't worth fighting over. Let's wait until we can have a civilized conservation about it." A one sided argument ends very quickly. In an argument, everyone feels that they are right and desires validation, regardless how loud they must speak and how vulgar their language must become to get their point across. By removing the tension and competition we save everyone time, energy, and dignity. Are we always wrong? Hell no! Do we need to prove ourselves correct in an argument? Equally, hell no! If everyone believes that they are right isn't everyone inherently just as wrong? Oh, the other cool caveat to this is, if the other person rekindles the same argument they are automatically the aggressor. (We can use that as leverage in the court of public opinion if needed- "I have no problem with them, but they wouldn't let it die.")

Saying things as nicely and personably as possible can be misconstrued. First of all, always be honest and direct. This is the only way people will know that they offended us, we caught their poor excuse, or we find them attractive and would like to explore further possibilities for a more serious relationship. Granted, my clients hire me and continually return to me because I am a no-nonsense, brutally honest, and direct person. One evaluator for my certification practicum called me a Howitzer (tank) with a sunflower in the barrel. I am powerful, big, and sometimes intimidating but I come from a place of pure empathy, curiosity, creativity, and care. Find your communication strengths and embrace them. Second, back up your honesty and directions with facts. Facts rule the world and opinions cloud the mind. By citing observations and known facts, we add instant credibility to our side of the conversation. Opinions, perceptions, projections, and expectations come from a place of personal weakness or bias. Opinions don't matter, to be honest. Life isn't a popularity contest; it's about results and facts. Yes, facts can be negative. At the time of this writing I'm 285 pounds (at the time of editing I'm already well below that). People call me fat. Yes, that's a negative outlook of a negative fact, however, it's an observable, quantifiable characteristic that I'm out of shape. I respond with, "Yes, thank you. I need to work on that. Have an awesome day." We can't argue with facts. If people approach me with opinions (usually start with "I think" or "I feel") such as "I think you're mean." I simply respond, "Thanks for your opinion. Have a great day." There's no point in arguing an opinion. They'll think they're right and, in keeping with the Independence Mantra, opinions have no bearing on us, anyways.

We are in charge of how our words affect others and how much they weigh on us. Proper communication skills (speaking) combined with exemplary listening skills will assist us in improving ourselves through networking and recruiting as well as assisting others by providing them exceptional service through proficient observation. Our ability to read people by listening to what they say, how they say it, and what they don't say (Triplex Listening) as well as observing what they do, how they do it, and what they don't do (Triplex Observation) provides us with facts that we can illustrate to others and explore in more depth to better understand how we can optimally serve them.

Own Yourself

I don't believe we could find two people more polar opposite than Gary Vaynerchuk and Mike Veny. Gary Vaynerchuk is a business and social media expert who is known for his blunt, often swear-laden observations of business and entrepreneurial action plans. Mike Veny is a suicide prevention and mental health advocate (as well as a fellow drummer) whose calm, soothing, and open approach to public speaking have opened up so many doors and hearts to breaking down the stigma of mental health challenges. I have learned very valuable lessons from these two men. The paramount lesson from both is to own who you are.

We all have a gift. Gary has an eye for human behavior as it relates to social media, marketing, and business practices. Mike has the ability to make people comfortable very quickly and to explain mental health challenges in a way that is very easy to understand and welcoming to questions. Both of these men know who they are, what their strengths are, and they are owning who they are to benefit the lives of others. When we take the time, patience, and energy to discover who we truly are and what our true gift is, we are setting ourselves up for success. There is an idiom that says, "If you love what you do for a living you'll never work a day in your life." The secret to loving what we're doing (first step is acknowledging that there *is* no secret) is to employ our gift in the service of others. Once we find what our gift is, we must find a way to turn our gift into a way to serve others.

How do we find our gift? It's going to sound stupid simple but the process begins with a genuine curiosity and a passion for finding our gift. Then, we have to look in the right places. If we believe our gift is in the automotive or transportation fields, then we probably don't need to pick up Better Homes & Gardens or watch the Food Network to find our gift. For instance, I knew I was called into coaching and assisting others to develop and achieve their goals. I threw myself into lectures, books, keynote speeches, and seminars about helping others. I never knew about life coaching but I knew I wanted to motivate, inspire, and lead people. I found my gift in the waning minutes of a presentation by Simon Sinek (One of my favorite authors, check him out!) speaking about Alcoholics Anonymous. He said the first step to recovery is acknowledging the problem- everyone knows that. It's even been parodied on television and in movies. However, the 12th step is the most crucial- it's service to others. A recovering alcoholic's 12th step is to assist another recovering alcoholic on their journey, BAM! My mental health challenges have been a journey of recovery. My 12th step- my service to others- is to assist others on their journey of recovery, management of mental health challenges, and the relentless pursuit of their desired results.

Be open to your gift. When I discovered mine I was equally excited and absolutely scared to death. I was very new on my journey and I did not feel equipped to help others. I didn't know how, when, or where I would help people, but I knew I had to kick my ass into gear to help myself first, then educate myself and share my knowledge and experience with others.

Monday Morning Quarterback

In retrospect, one shortcoming in my approach to handling my situation was that I gave up at every roadblock. I would talk with one teacher, one administrator at a time and accept that they would take care of things with blind faith. They were adults. They were in positions of power. They would get things done when they got around to it. If they didn't do anything I would accept defeat for that day. I was naïve in that I expected everyone to put forth their best effort and accepted *any* effort as "the best they could do." I was taught not to disrespect people and not to question authority. "Shopping" for results, or going from one teacher to another until I got the answer or action I desired was seen as disrespectful and a show of no confidence. I didn't want to go against my upbringing and I didn't want to upset my teachers.

The proper approach in dire situations like I was in is almost completely opposite to what I actually did. If we don't get the answers, actions, or results we desire or, in this case need, then we must continue to seek out those results as quickly as possible. This piece isn't just about bullying or my specific situation, this applies to any big goals or desired results we have in any area of our life. Don't fear or worry about hurting the feelings of others when it comes to seeking results. If we're not seeing the hustle, commitment, effort, and most importantly results we desire and expect, then we definitely reserve the right and, honestly, we owe it to ourselves to find the person or people who are able to deliver the desired results as efficiently and effectively as possible.

Policies, procedures, and protocols to address bullying, harassment, and assault in schools have drastically and dramatically improved since I was in school. Teachers have been put on notice and they are trained and equipped to be much more aware, observant, and reactive of the signs of bullying and harassment and they are plugged into the students far more. If my situation were to play out in modern times (social media not withstanding) I would have been sent to the office by the first teacher I spoke with, a detailed report would have been taken, Leader and the followers would have been called down and interviewed immediately, all of the parents would be have been called and notified, and the police may have been involved. However, for the sake of being complete and thorough, it is wise to remind teachers, counselors, coaches, friends, colleagues, and parents to take accusations very seriously especially when presented with physical evidence. Do not be hesitant or afraid to push the accusations up the chain of command until the issue has been properly resolved.

Some, if not all of you, will have hesitations about being a rat, snitch, or tattletale like I was. This was twofold because I was worried equally about my reputation and the retaliation I would face from Leader and the followers. However, I was doing myself a disservice by not focusing on what I'll call preservation of life- or minimizing physical, emotional, and mental injury. In the same breath my hesitations shouldn't have precluded the teachers and certainly not the administrators from taking action to stop the abuse. Thankfully, checks and balances have been put in place to monitor the situations and schools are much more vigilant and proactive when it comes to nipping that kind of behavior in the bud.

Improving Children from the Inside

I allowed my value to be determined by others. I wanted and needed outward affirmation in order to accept myself. My grandparents and parents told me that "it's what's on the inside that counts," but never explained it. It is essential that we take the time to quantify, qualify, and validate our children. By providing tangible evidence that they are awesome in our eyes (and not taking anything- academic, musical, or athletic performance- for granted) and helping them to plan their goals and dreams will carry them much farther than any present wrapped for a birthday or holiday. I believe that Cameron Carpenter, the extraordinary organist, said it best when he was asked what parents can do for their children. He begged and pleaded that parents just get out of their children's way. I believe he holds a strong point. Children are so susceptible to influence, especially from their parents and other family members. Our imaginations and the outer limits of our mind are only corralled and blockaded by the stagnant and concrete minds of authoritative adults who have been conditioned to "think realistically." If we truly allowed our children to pursue what intrigues and fascinates them, I'm convinced they will find something they are truly passionate about. If they are truly passionate about something and love every nuance and detail of the matter then they will most likely see their career as a hobby and will garner much happiness and enjoyment from it. As the old saying goes, "If you love what you do, you'll never work a day in your life." After all, isn't our only hope for our children to be happy, healthy, and well?

Why is there so much nastiness in our society? Where did it come from? We are- we have become- an extrinsically, socially, outwardly centered society. We are superficial. If what we present on the outside isn't good enough for everyone else, then *we* are not good enough. We are fat, we are ugly, we're too slow, we're too weak, we have wrinkles, we have cellulite, we don't wear the right shoes, pants, shirt, underwear, cologne, we don't eat the right food or drink the right drink, or drive the right car. Why? Because someone else *said so!* And that's complete and utter nonsense!

So how can we work to rectify this? How do we get away from this extrinsically, socially, outwardly centered culture? We fall back. We fall back into ourselves. This is difficult. This will take time. We need to develop a safe, secure, nurturing environment in ourselves where we will be protected. I never felt totally safe within myself because I always let the outside in. If we leave our doors unlocked people and animals we don't want in there are going to get in over time and it will eventually and inevitably fall into disrepair; things will get stolen and broken, everything will be dirty, and it will not remain whole for very long. If we leave ourselves open and unprotected to the outside world, we will not remain whole for very long, either.

Eliminating Opinions

In my other book, *The Skeleton Key,* I discuss ideas of
eliminating opinions, writing our own story, finding our true
calling in life, and treating ourselves well. I don't want to take
up too much time repeating what is in that book but I'll give a
quick overview to tie it all together. My model, the Power
Chamber, (I joke that every personal development book has to
have an annoying, obnoxious model name) consists of the
Essence, Center, Role, Independence Mantra, and Reciprocal
Golden Rule. The Essence is who we are boiled down to our
simplest values and mission. The meaning of essence is the
most concentrated form of something. For instance,
concentrated orange juice is still orange juice. It has all the
elements of orange juice but it has been condensed down to
eliminate the liquid. All we must do to restore the OJ to its full
state is add water and stir. The process of putting our Essence
into motion is a bit more in depth. For me, my Essence is
"service of others." It is what dictates the direction we travel
through life and our anchor point when times get tough. Our
Center is our "why." Channeling my inner Simon Sinek (His
book, *Start with Why,* is where this concept is derived.), it is
why we are who we are and *why* we do what we do. We all
have reasons, which are connected to our Essence, for our
mission and our desired results. The Role is our actions. It is

how we are who we are and *how* we do what we do. We are totally in control of who we are and how we act. It boils down to how much work we are willing to put in and how strong we are to withstand the criticisms of others to become who we want to be and do what we want to do. This dovetails well with the Independence Mantra (I'm sure glad I designed it that way!) which states that opinions don't mean anything.

Opinions others hold about us, opinions we hold of others, and even opinions we hold of ourselves come from perceptions, projections, biases, judgments, fears, and predispositions taught to us and learned by us when we were much younger. Hell, sometimes these opinions are decades old and have no factual basis in modern times but we are conditioned to believe that they do (i.e. racism). By forming our own evaluations based on facts that we have observed (opinions are not based on facts, but emotions) we can dictate, manage, and leverage our beliefs of ourselves and others to propel us forward out of our comfort zone. Our beliefs lead to our actions and the Independence Mantra leads to the Reciprocal Golden Rule. The Reciprocal Golden Rule creates an intrinsic, inward, self-care component to offset the Golden Rule which states "Treat others as you wish to be treated." By treating ourselves how we wish to be treated and how we treat others we not only provide a standard regarding how we expect others to treat us, but also ensure that our needs are being addressed at least on a personal level.

When our needs are met we can charge our batteries by being served and fulfilled. It allows us to serve and fulfill others more fully. I firmly believe that we all serve one another regardless of what we do. When we invest time and energy on ourselves it makes the time and energy we spend on others rarer, and thus, a more valuable commodity. It also prepares us to enter this time of service of others with a full tank, clear head, and caring heart.

Teach Children to Defend Themselves

I'll be honest, I'm not just talking about martial arts, or boxing, or physical protection, but they very certainly apply. Hear me out: as many books as I'll write, as many presentations as I'll have the opportunity to give, bullying and abuse will continue far beyond my last day here on Earth. Police officers know bad guys have weapons so they trained to use their weapons-their mind, voice, body, and physical weapons. Firefighters know that fire is hot and it will burn them so they wear special gear and they train their bodies rigorously to prevent fatigue and injury in the direst, most volatile of times. If we know people suck (not everyone, but there's always one person in the crowd- and plenty of weak minded people to follow them) shouldn't we take protective measures against the harm we face from others?

In addition to staying physically active, mentally disciplined, and able to defend ourselves physically if the need arises, I also believe that a strong defense starts with a good offense. Having long term goals to pursue, creating visions, and making mini game plans are great ways to establish an anchor in something bigger and greater than ourselves. Future plans give us something to work for. If we're going to be the best damn rock drummer in the world who cares what negative things a classmate has to say? *Dude, say those things to me when you have to pay $150 to get into my concert. ... Then I'll smile, shake your hand, and thank you for coming to the show!* (That's a bit more of a "middle finger" way of saying, "You're right, I'm sorry.")

Speak Up, Sound Off

Veterans who have served in active war zones have different terms for engaging in battles with the enemy. My friends who served valiantly in Operation Enduring Freedom and Operation Iraqi Freedom have called it "Seeing contact," while the Vietnam War veterans I have had the privilege of speaking with have called it "Being in the shit." Whatever the case may be, it refers to being incessantly bombarded with munitions while trying to defend and protect themselves. In a harassment, abuse, or bullying situation where there is a pack mentality such as my case with Leader and the followers, it can certainly feel like we're "in the shit."

In any basic training or academy we are taught that communication is essential for survival. If we're moving, reloading, or doing anything other than firing then we should be talking. The same is true when we're in an abusive situation. If we're out of energy- out of ammo, so to speak- and we need back up, then we must talk to anyone and everyone until we find our back up. I lamented that one of my downfalls was that I was timid and didn't want to inconvenience anyone. The reality is that if no one knows, no one can help. The best way to help yourself in situations like I was in is to find someone else to help you. Do *not* be ashamed or feel less human. Only the strongest people are strong enough to ask for help. That is why the most successful people are the ones that I have reached out to work with someone else.

As I mentioned in *"Look for the Helpers,"* there are people all around us who are ready, willing, and able to help. We have neighbors, our parents, siblings, teachers, members of our faith community at church, coaches, and parents of friends to turn to. *Someone* will definitely be ready to step up and take charge. This is where finding someone to invest in us is so important. If we want to invest the time and energy to seek someone's assistance in a serious situation then they need to invest their time and energy by assisting us in getting the help and support that we need. No matter how many people it takes, we must keep asking until we find the support that we need. Know that you can always call or email me for support and assistance. My email address is AJ@CrushComplacency.com.

Altering our beliefs can be a long, intense, arduous process but it is certainly worthwhile. The basis for this exercise is that we have learned everything but haven't made a conscious decision to employ or eliminate that belief or teaching. In *The Skeleton Key* I talked about the realms of mastery: the eight areas of our lives that we have the opportunity to learn about and evaluate, as well as leverage, alter, and manipulate in order to get the most out of this life. Quickly, those realms on are the Inner Self realm, which consists of the mental, higher thinking portion of ourselves. This is essentially our own character development. The Outer Self realm, which speaks to our physical body, its condition, and its appearance. The Physical realm, which is the immediate world we live in. This includes our living space, vehicle, and workspace. The Professional realm speaks to our current employment as well as our desired employment which we are pursuing. The Spiritual realm is however we are able to find peace within ourselves and the world we live in. This can be through God, nature, meditation, or any other personal means, as long as it doesn't inflict harm on oneself or others. The Social realm, which consists of the world outside of our Physical realm in which we interact with others. This is often an area that experiences great development and expansion because our high expectations of ourselves usually translate into higher expectations of those surrounding us. The Familial realm is our inner circle that includes our personal handpicked mastermind group that I referred to as our Executive Board. Finally, the Financial realm consists of our present financial situation as well as our desired financial situation that we are pursuing.

Establishing our beliefs consists of going through all the realms and documenting what our beliefs are about that realm. Then, we evaluate our environmental beliefs and decide where we learned that belief and if we wish to keep it or- and this is important- replace it with a better, more productive believe. We can't delete a belief without installing a new, preferably opposite and empowering belief, in its place.

Scary Numbers: Evening the Odds

The world is full of scary numbers. The 12 through 26-year-old age bracket accounts for 95% of eating disorders[6]. The second leading cause of death among people ages 10-24 is suicide[7]. This is disturbing to me because eating disorders immediately jumped out as "body image" and "control" oriented behaviors. Following suit, this means that children and young adults in this age bracket have some serious challenges negotiating who they are, who they want to be, where they are, where they want to go, and what healthy behavior consists of. These kids- whoever they are to us: classmate, sibling, niece or nephew, friend, teammate, a friend's kid, or neighbor- need our help. People, especially kids, aren't born with language identifying fat, ugly, and other nasty, hateful terms. They also don't know how to organize those terms in the "negative" category. All that information is taught and subsequently learned as we're growing up. We

---

[6] Futures Palm Beach. 2016. Anorexia Facts and Statistics.
http://www.futuresofpalmbeach.com/anorexia-treatment/facts-statistics/
[7] Jason Foundation, Inc. 2016. Youth Suicide Statistics.
http://jasonfoundation.com/prp/facts/youth-suicide-statistics/

learn how to label, we learn how to hate, we learn how to isolate, and we learn how to break people down. Yes, this is all true. However, if we can learn all that horrible behavior we can learn positive behaviors to counteract all the negative people in the world.

We can alter the behavior of those around us by constantly and consistently modeling proper, positive behavior. By always exhibiting kind, positive behavior that uplifts those around us, others are going to take notice and at least log that type of behavior into their memory banks. As time progresses, we will build up the rapport of being the positive person and we can slowly, carefully begin to question people on the reasons why they call other people names or have negative perceptions of certain groups. Most likely, they have learned these views and behaviors from someone they hold dear and see these beliefs as "normal." Remember, normal is malleable and can change as our environment changes- and we have full creative license to alter our environment at will, especially regarding our beliefs.

Employee Assistance

Employers, you are an important, no, an *ESSENTIAL* part of this equation. Everyone that does business in any industry- from food services to office work, to education, and everyone in between- needs to pay attention to their staff. Strictly from a cold, heartless business standpoint, if your staff is not well then your business is not well. Your staff, your workers represent your company and they are the lifeblood of your business. I firmly believe that yearly psychological screenings for *everyone* in local, county, state, and federal public service should be mandatory. Police, fire, EMS, doctors, correction officers, dispatchers, nurses, and all public servants deal with mind boggling amounts of stress and they deserve the best medical and mental health services in return for the services they render.

I know the policies and procedures of the Massachusetts Department of Correction best, so I will use them as an example. In Massachusetts state prisons, if an inmate claims crisis (usually after they are locked in their cell) we are instructed to post up in front of their cell and advise our direct supervisor of the situation. From there, the inmate is escorted to the Health Services Unit (hospital) where they are assessed by a Licensed Mental Health Clinician (or a properly trained nurse if a LMHC is unavailable) and placed on the hospital ward for observation. More recently, they have moved to calling medical emergency codes in order to get the inmate mental health services even faster. If an officer expresses similar symptoms or feelings of crisis we are laughed at by coworkers, told to harden up, and handle that situation on our own time. That may not be what is on the books, but that is what has happened inside the facilities in the past. In our policies and in our prison culture it is alluded to and suggested that, as long as inmate suicides go down or remain the same, we're good. If the officers' suicide rates go up, that's just the price of doing business.

There was a stretch when I returned to the Massachusetts Department of Correction in mid-2011 through mid-2012 that we had our mourning bands on our badges more often than not. If my memory and research serve me right, my institution buried seven officers that year, four were from suicide or accidental deaths. There was no bump in mental health services for officers. There were no massive studies done to find out what was happening to the officers, but there was one conducted for inmates. But hey, at least we got a two-hour presentation at our yearly in-service training on how to recognize the symptoms of depression in coworkers. For people like me, who had to hide my diagnosis for a long time out of fear I would be removed from my assignment, or ridiculed by administration and coworkers, that was just a Role, a script I was given on how to act to avoid being caught. However, I didn't need to really worry about being caught because no one really paid attention to anyone else, anyways.

(I am pleased to have to correct myself that, at the time of this writing a study is being conducted in Massachusetts and Nebraska to monitor correction staff suicides and mental health care statistics in the top two most effected states.)

The discussion is not relegated to just corrections. Police, fire, EMS, dispatchers, nurses, and doctors who observe and deal with traumatic scenes on a daily basis are called public servants. We take oaths to protect and serve our communities.

We put ourselves in harm's way, see things people should never have to see, and most of us do things or have done things no one should ever have to do. We keep ourselves in check and compartmentalize the stress, anguish, fear, and anxiety because we are taught to maintain discipline, focus, and professionalism at all times. It is this ability that makes us good at our jobs. It is the inability to decompartmentalize things that makes us vulnerable and susceptible to Post Traumatic Stress Disorder, anxiety, depression and suicidal thoughts, substance abuse, and other mental health challenges.

Decompartmentalization (The Art of Self Care)

Destressing, decompartmentalizing, relaxation, or self-care-however we identify taking time away from the hustle, bustle, and business of our lives is of paramount concern. Before I begin I want to address the men. Guys, I need you to turn down the testosterone for a few minutes and put that false macho-man bravado garbage in your back pocket. Women live longer than us for a reason and, though I'm not an expert, I am willing to bet part of it is because we tend to handle stress about as well as we handle anyone questioning the size of our shmenzer. What we in Western culture see as "pampering" ourselves is viewed as normal self care in other countries like we view but brushing our teeth and washing our hands.

I like to evaluate every day in a vacuum- meaning yesterday is gone and tomorrow isn't here yet- and see what progress I made towards my goals and how I can improve my performance tomorrow. This way, whether I have a horrible day or an absolutely amazing day I can put a cap on it and strive for a better day tomorrow. Also, loving yourself and your body in a caring way is therapeutic. Giving ourselves a manicure/ pedicure is a great way to improve hygiene while reducing stress. Guys, that means you, too. We must learn how to take care of our hands, feet, and nails. Our significant others don't appreciate Joe Dirt or Edward Scissorhands caressing and their body. It's actually very therapeutic, calming, and helps with self-esteem (weird, I know, but trust me on this). I struggled with biting my nails for a very long time. Looking forward to the soothing and calming effects of a manicure helped me to gain and maintain the discipline needed to break that horrible, dirty habit. My other guilty pleasure is a nice soak in a very hot bath with bath oils. I clean my bathroom from ceiling to floor and every crack in between once a week. That night, I draw a bath as hot as I can stand it with some bath oils, and just soak my bones for a while. Sometimes, my thoughts are on the week that went by. Sometimes my thoughts are focused on how I'll be the next Tony Robbins with a worldwide brand and an island in the South Pacific. Other times my thoughts are… *It's already been 45 minutes?! That was fast!* Whatever your practices are and wherever your thoughts go, it's important to take time to rest and repair your body and mind on the regular basis.

An Exploration of Faith & Mental Health

Religion is a dicey subject to begin with, but when we add in a discussion or exploration of mental health care and suicide… well, I'd rather juggle butchers' knives with Vaseline on my hands. However, as a teenager in middle school growing up in an ultraconservative Catholic family, mental health was not talked about. It wasn't talked about because "No one in this family is crazy." Much like most things in my childhood, mental health was a binary, black-and-white topic; you're either sane and fully functioning or clinically insane and institutionalized. I needed a resource that would give me the truth, the whole truth, and nothing but the truth… and in this case "So help me God" is very applicable. I never found that resource because I never asked for it. I believe this had a two-part causation. I was too chicken, embarrassed, and ashamed to talk to anyone about the abuse, so I don't think I was capable of asking for help at that point. The other cause was that requesting information about *anything* in school was treated as an admission of guilt and was met with scorn rather than the requested information. Asking about condoms and STDs? You're obviously sexually active and must be counseled on the church's teaching of abstinence. Asking about the dangers of smoking? You're definitely chain-smoking like George Burns.

Since I am well aware that I wasn't the only person that was in need of sound information back then and I'm not naïve or narrow minded enough to think that the problem has been rectified, I took it upon myself to research and investigate the most modern stances I could find from the major religions. I did this partially out of curiosity and partially to dispel the rumors, or what I hoped were rumors, that all religions hold a hyper conservative and narrow-minded approach to mental health and steadfast, unwavering interpretations of suicide. I must make it very clear that, although I obtained the assistance of a Catholic Priest, Jewish Rabbi, and Muslim Imam to assist me in locating websites, journal articles, and books that accurately represented the respective faith's position on mental health care and suicide, I am not a theological scholar and my interpretation of the literature may not coincide with the official doctrine. All of the religious leaders and scholars that I spoke with requested that I strongly encourage anyone that needs to talk should feel open and comfortable approaching their religious leaders to ask for guidance and advice.

I believe this is a good time to reiterate the concept of "Seeking Your Yes." If you'll recall, this concept centers around the idea of talking with anyone and everyone through any means necessary until we receive the action or information that we desire. Although our religious leaders *represent* the deity we worship here on earth, it doesn't mean that they are infallible or properly equipped to handle such a stressful and sensitive concern. The best resources I found for information were websites specifically designed for mental health awareness, education, and contact for every religion. Their responses were fast, informative, and supportive. Simply conduct an online search for your religion's mental health support. For example, I searched for "Christian Mental Health

Support" and I was instantly connected to many reputable, responsive, and supportive organizations that are rooted in the teachings and compassion of my faith.

Since I'm Catholic and I feel most comfortable addressing my faith, I'll start there. When I was growing up I was told that if a person died by suicide they did not receive a funeral mass or any graveside ceremony. They were not given last rights (also known as the sacrament of Anointing of the Sick), they did not go to heaven and they did not receive salvation. In short, "Go directly to jail. Do not pass GO. Do not collect $200." Sadly, this hard line, ultraconservative viewpoint was accepted and practiced for a very long time. In fact, this practice ended only in 1983 via a decree by Pope Saint John Paul II[8]. Now, Catholics, and to the fullest of my knowledge, all Christians that die via suicide are able to be buried from their churches with full burial ceremonies. As more knowledge and understanding of mental health challenges has become more publicized and widely accepted, the Catholic Church has amended their views considerably in recent years. Pope Francis stated, in only the second week of his papacy, that the church has to be welcoming to an understanding of all people saying, "Who am I to judge?" He also cited the Gospel of John (8:7) which says, "He who is without sin among you, let him be the first to throw a stone."

To kill a person, including oneself, is seen as a violation of the commandment "Thou shall not kill." In doing so, it is also a cardinal sin or mortal sin in which the church believes that that person's relationship with God is severed. Pretty cut and dry. If someone killed me I'd want God to be like, "Dude, I made him. He's a one-of-a-kind model. No, we're not friends anymore." However, "for a sin to be mortal it must have three characteristics. It is a gravely wrong action. The person knew

[8] Stuart, James. "Funerals Due to Suicide & the Roman Catholic Church." People of Our Every Day Life. Retrieved from http://peopleof.oureverydaylife.com/funerals-due-suicide-roman-catholic-church-2612.html

it was gravely wrong. The person did so out of free will.[9]"
This is where the church used to jump to the conclusion that
people were in control of their actions and decisions 100% of
the time unless they were committed to a mental institution
but has retracted its old-school train of thought. As
understanding of mental health challenges has begun to
permeate our society more, the church has backed off its
stance and has recognized that, in order to get to the point of
killing oneself, a person is most likely not in their "right
mind." This negates the idea of suicide being committed under
free will, and thus, no longer a mortal sin.

Judaism has followed a very similar path to Christianity in
terms of recognizing mental health challenges and negotiating
suicide. In my perusal of the articles forwarded to me by my
local Rabbi, I found many references to ultraconservative,
very old (turn of the 20th century) documents that flatly
denied funeral rites to anyone that was even suspected of
committing suicide. In much the same fashion, as I delve
deeper in scholarly articles, interviews, keynote speeches, and
lectures I found the rhetoric was softening to be kinder and
more accepting of those challenged by mental illnesses, as
well as discussions of education and removing the stigma
around the challenges.

Seeking mental health care is supported and encouraged
by the Jewish faith, supplemented by a suggestion to increase
religious studies and communication with the faithful
community. As more and more people in the Jewish
community raise their hand to be counted as one challenged
by mental health illnesses, it appears that the community is
swarming them with support, understanding, and most
importantly, faith-based resources.

Although suicide is, as expected, greatly admonished in
the Jewish faith, I have found a little concession. The

---

[9] Does the Catholic Church teach that anyone who commits suicide goes to hell?
(N.d.) Retrieved from http://catholicbridge.com/catholic/suicide-hell-catholic-
teaching.php

treatment of one who died by suicide is very hands off, as with the early Christian church. No funeral service, no eulogy, and they are not allowed to be buried in a Jewish cemetery. Now, in an article[10] I found a glimmer of hope. It states that mental health challenges take away some of the sting of a suicide. Furthermore, it has become customary for local Torah authorities to be more lenient in terms of interpreting the situation. It appears that, in the case of a sudden unattended death, a grave accident is assumed to be the root cause of death unless there is some significant, undeniable evidence that a suicide was intended and executed.

I had the most difficulty finding information about the acceptance of mental health care and treatment of suicide in the Muslim faith. As with Judaism and Christianity, Islam strictly forbids suicide. It is seen as against the will of Allah and the teachings of the Qur'an. With that said, I found evidence that the funeral prayers should be recited for the deceased, though they shall not be conducted by the imam. I read several reflections that stated that people that died by suicide were given full burial rights because of a known mental health challenge or no one witnessed the suicide. I interpret the lack of a witness to parallel the Jewish assumption of a grave accident in the event of a sudden unattended death. Another source[11] stated that suicide is not a *kufr* (grave sin resulting in eternal hellfire) and would not render the person a *Kufir* (a non-Muslim; i.e. excommunicated from the Church of Islam due to their actions). The Imam's response to the question goes on to say that if there is evidence of mental illness resulting in "loss of reason" then the act of suicide is not considered a sin and it is believe that "The Pen has been lifted from three: from the sleeper until he awakens, from the child until he reaches puberty and from the insane

---

[10] Jacob, W., Kravitz, L., Plaut, W., et al. *90. A Eulogy for a Suicide.* (1980). Retrieved from http://ccarnet.org/responsa/arr-306-307/
[11] Saalih al-Munajjid, Shaykh Muhammad. 146375: She became mentally ill. (2011, January 06) Retrieved from https://islamqa.info/en/146375

person until he comes to his senses -- or until he comes round." (Book #40, Hadith #4403)

Mental health care is a *very* dicey topic in Islam. More conservative Imams believe that there is no such thing as mental health challenges, but rather a lack of faith and inattentiveness to Allah and the Qur'an. There appears to be a movement among younger Muslims that is more accepting of mental health care in conjunction with increased prayers and studies in an attempt to weaken the stigma. Again, this parallels the Jewish approach of speaking with the faithful community, seeking mental health care, and supplementing the care with increased religious studies and devout prayer. Speaking and corresponding with younger Imams, I get the impression that the winds of change are swirling in this new generation of Muslim leaders to be more accepting and supportive of mental health needs in their faith community.

Again, I am not a religious scholar, I am human, and I may have misinterpreted some doctrine. This is meant to open the lines of communication within and amongst the religions to develop a comprehensive response and acceptance of mental health challenges. I invite all religious leaders and scholars to contact me to correct or reinforce the views I have put forth here. I never intended to be a focal point for suicide prevention and awareness or mental health care perspectives regarding the different faiths but, if that's my part in making this world a better place then sign me up. Let's talk, let's invite others in on the discussion, and let's break the stigma of mental health challenges and suicide prevention together.

Disclaimer: The following views are mine and mine alone. They have not been reviewed, filtered, or approved of by any religious leader of any faith.

Going with the "Power Chamber" template (my model in "The Skeleton Key), we can look at religion or culture as a pseudo-Role. Take this with a grain of salt. I'm not saying culture and religion are bad in any way. What I *am* saying is that religion and culture are a part of who we are and can be encompassed in our personal Role without infringing on our opportunity to seek treatment.

Whatever religion we believe in, or if you don't believe in God let's just say nature (but let's use God for a generally accepted term, for now) I believe that whoever or whatever we believe in just wants us to be happy. Also, we are seeking treatment with the goal of assisting others which is an incredible step forward and a step up in our ability to serve others. Seeking help to assist in rebuilding and improving ourselves is a means to becoming happy and productive. Furthermore, I would have to say that a God that cares about his or her creation would certainly appreciate and condone not only someone wanting to help themselves but also the person who is empathetic and compassionate to the needs of others.

Any faith that knowingly and willfully ostracizes or judges those who have mental health challenges needs to be disassembled. The intention of religion, as I see it, is to unify people in a close knit community to help everyone grow and progress together. (Wow, that sounds incredibly similar to what I'm trying to accomplish through this book. I hope I'm not coming off as preachy.) If your religion or faith is not meeting your needs then you must have the courage, confidence, and- for lack of a better phrase- faith in yourself to seek your spiritual yes elsewhere.

My Challenges &
Their Value

I'll openly disclose that, for a split second, the top of this page read "What Mental Health Challenges I Have and What They Mean to Me" but I smartened up before I even finished writing that. In short, my original diagnoses were primary Post Traumatic Stress Disorder, depression, and anxiety. I'll take you through all of that and the updates but, generally speaking, all three go hand in hand when dealing with traumatic events that happen to an individual.

There are degrees for every diagnosis (or at least most that I have researched) just like there are different degrees of burns and different severities of headaches for physical ailments. Primary PTSD is when some trauma happens to the person directly. This trauma can be physical, verbal, or emotional and it must have recurring, long-lasting properties. To relate it to my own story, I held onto many details in this book for approximately 18 years before seeking therapy. Even more details started bubbling up when I started to write about what happened. This is what our brain does- it works very hard to avoid pain. If avoiding pain means that our brain takes a skeleton- for lack of a better term since pain can take many forms (it's different for everyone) and buries it very far down into our subconscious where it'll be hard to access, then that's what the brain will do.

Anxiety is "a feeling of worry, nervousness, or unease, typically about an imminent event or something with an uncertain outcome.[12]" For someone who values certainty (like myself) this is a challenge. This is what I mean when I say that I believe most people have mental health challenges at some level. The definition of anxiety comes up in conversation at least once a day for me. I think our society is at fault for a large portion of this issue but that's best left for a book that is still in the planning stages. Worrying about an outcome seems to be a general mindset for some people. When I think of the phrase "what if..." several faces pop in my mind. If this is you and you aren't seeing a therapist, please consider making the call. It's totally worth the co-pay and you can thank me later.

One very inconvenient truth about anxiety is that it makes us question everything... Everything! Anxiety causes people to irrationally question aspects of their lives. Irrationally generally means "Against rationale." Rationale generally means "A logical basis for an action." Therefore, irrationally means "against a logical basis for an action," which is probably a good indicator why anxiety is a mental health disorder. One area of my life that was severely impacted by my anxiety was my relationships. I have only had two relationships since I entered college in 2002. Both lasted well over two years and both look very promising for long-term success from the outside. Inside, however, my mind was performing a gymnastics routine worthy of an Olympic gold medal. After about the six-month mark in both relationships, I began to question everything about myself and the girl.

---

[12] Anxiety. 2015. In OxfordDictionaries.*com*. Retrieved August 18, 2015, from
http://www.oxforddictionaries.com/us/definition/american_english/anxiety

Everything was phrased in a negative tone and my logic- or lack thereof- lead to a very negative place

"She's too good for me. I don't deserve her. Does she realize that she's too good for me? Does she see that there are far better options out there?"

I found myself keeping mental score, charting how each guy she talked to was better than me and posed a threat to our relationship. Anytime my girlfriend changed her hairstyle or got a new article of clothing I braced for impact and forecasted the worst possible scenario. I recall meeting my girlfriend for lunch one day and she arrived in a short jean skort (skirt with shorts built in), a halter top, and had just had her belly button pierced. She look like a complete knockout but my mind instantly catastrophized the whole scene. *"Dude, this isn't for you! She has to be eying up other guys. You don't deserve to be with anyone looking that good. She's going to realize that she deserves a better guy any day now."* I found myself getting insanely and uncontrollably jealous for (looking back) absolutely asinine reasons. So yes, anxiety sucks, but it can be controlled with therapy and a lot of internal work.

Depression is when we lose interest or desire in daily activities for an extended period of time. Major depressive disorder has a timeline of two weeks. Depression is usually linked to the loss of a loved one or significant defeat in life but it can be seasonal or chemically influenced. I immediately pick up on "adjustable" terms such as "significant" because the term can change from person-to-person. When we have a loss of desire to engage in an activity that we usually love we have to ask ourselves "Why?" If the answer is deeper than anticipated, then it may be time to take appropriate actions.

After many months of working methodically and diligently to improve myself through reading books, listening to audio programs, watching keynote speeches and seminars, and countless hours of meditation, mindfulness, journaling, reflection, planning, writing, and attending weekly therapy, things started to turn around in a big way. I have managed my

PTSD to the point where is very difficult to cause a memory to spark up or unconsciously sabotage a moment in the present. My situational specific anxiety has been reassessed or downgraded to general anxiety disorder, and my depression has been downgraded to dysthymia- which is a very mild case of depression. I call it "depression light."

As we can see, mental health challenges don't merely go away. In fact, there has been a few times during the writing of this book that I needed to take a step back, console my inner child, and assure myself that what's being brought up is in the past and we are in a safe environment. At some points- especially "Losing My Compass," "New Weapons II," and "The Ugly Truth,"- it was a dicey, touch-and-go process that took me days to methodically get through the pieces. I believe part of the reason for my dramatic turn is that I've wanted to help others so badly my whole life and I can only help others if I am at my best. I've had a taste of the good life with less depression, less anxiety, and hardly any incidents of PTSD and I want to remain there and even improve my situation even more.

PART VI: CLOSURE

Final Approach

So what have I learned from therapy and how has it helped me? I've learned that bad things happen to good people sometimes *because* they are good people and others see kindness as a weakness. I've learned that kindness isn't a weakness but one of the greatest strengths there is. I've learned to love again- myself, my family, and others. I've learned not to hold back, to make a plan, and go for it. Nothing is good or bad. Everything is just information and WE assign the value to it through emotions and feelings. Make a decision, take action, adjust your behavior, and take action again. I've learned to communicate better and to evaluate things from my perspective and the perspective of others. I've learned to replace that box of darkness with the tools of enlightenment- my Center, the Independence Mantra, and the Reciprocal Golden Rule. But most of all, I've learned there's a helluva lot to live for.

If you'll recall I started this book by saying, "I have had a plan to kill myself since I was twelve years old." I'd like an opportunity to amend that. I *had* a plan to kill myself since I was 12. That plan has been replaced with a plan and commitment to help others seek help without judgment and fear so they, too, can be as happy and fulfilled as I am.

Going Public &
The Other Side of Vulnerability

I have been nervous and anxious about sharing my story in public for a long time. Sure, I've done presentations at my church and for some smaller groups, but those were confined audiences expecting information wrapped into a story. Making a public spectacle and willfully putting my painful, sensitive information out in the public form- especially the cesspool known as social media- had me wound tighter than my favorite snare drum. That was one thing on my "Goals for 2016" list that was quickly approaching and exponentially jacking up my stress and anxiety levels: World Suicide Prevention Day, September 10th. The plan was to make a canned video (scripted, edited, formatted- not totally impromptu an off-the-cuff) detailing the general ideas I've addressed here.

I spent two days writing out, editing, censoring, and re-writing what I wanted to address and how, specifically, I wanted to say it. I ran the script by a few clients, licensed mental health clinicians, and suicide prevention advocates to suggest edits to my word choices and what information I should add or omit. I cut the first draft of the video and sent it to a few friends. I would cut three more versions of the 12-minute long address making small changes to word choices, pictures I used of my grandfather, and changes to lighting, camera angle, and other small details only I really picked up on along the way.

Next, I had a list of prominent people and groups that I would share my video with in hopes that they'd get behind my story and share it with their community. All in all, I would share the video on over 30 pages. I invited approximately 50 people to a secret group on Facebook to be the first people see the video and, hopefully, share it with their networks, as well. Some of you may think that all that preparation work was a great PR move to get more views and spread the video far and wide. Well, that was partially the idea and the projected result, but the main motivation was to paint myself into a corner that I could only get out of by sharing the video.

I quit the project at least five times. I could totally wait until next year! I'm not ready. I don't want to deal with it. I'm going to get kicked out of my position at the prison. This is relationship napalm. Anyone who sees this will want nothing to do with me. All of the self-doubt, self-loathing, negative "Andy" mentality talk was floating to the surface and it was difficult to block it out and concentrate.

I made a card and kept it on my nightstand, desk, kitchen table, kitchen counter, bathroom, and in my car. I saw it everywhere and it re-centered me every time I saw it. It reminded me of the purpose, the emotional reason I was doing this- my "WHY." It simply said "You want to be a leader… F**king LEAD!"

The night before the video went live I made sure everything was ready. My list of pages and people that the video was being sent to was set out on my desk with a pen by it to cross them off. My messages for Facebook, Twitter, and Instagram were written in a Word document so I could just cut, paste, and post. The video was already uploaded and scheduled for 7 AM EST. Other than deleting the video from YouTube, this train was ready to ride.

At that moment I felt in eerie sense of calm. I was at ease with everything and resigned myself to whatever was in store for me on the other side. All the stressing, pacing, hemming and hawing, laboring over word choices, and worrying about how others would react was gone. It was replaced by an almost robotic business approach of following the protocol for what needed to happen. If I was going to put myself out there and share the dirtiest, ugliest, most vulnerable piece of my past then I may as well get as many eyeballs on this is possible. I formulated a plan that I would do the initial launch work then only check social media twice during the day- once at lunch and once at the end of the night. The rest of the day would be spent keeping as busy and productive as possible.

A strange thing happened at the end of the night. Sure, I had a few messages, the video got a lot of response from my close friends, and I made a lot of great connections in the mental health and bullying prevention fields. However, something more important happened. I gained a lot of clarity by exiting my Comfort Zone in such a big way and making myself so vulnerable and emotionally available.

I learned three major things in the coming days after my video was released. The first, I've already alluded to- what was vulnerable in uncharted territory was now the new normal. Ralph Waldo Emerson wrote, "The mind, once stretched by a new idea, never returns to its original dimensions." I firmly believe that this holds true for our Comfort Zone, as well. As of September 10, 2016 at 7 AM EST what was a closely guarded secret was now a story of strength, perseverance, and a witness to the power of proper mental health care and a call for bullying advocacy that had been seen by hundreds across the United States and even as far as Africa and the Middle East.

Secondly, I got to employ Triplex Observation (watching 1) what people do, 2) how they do it [attitudes/ emotions], and 3) what they don't do) in a big way. I was able to clearly see and learn who is with me for the long haul and who is just with me for the ride. Steve Harvey tells the story in his book *Act Like a Success, Think Like a Success* (which I highly recommend) about all of us pulling our own wagon (like Oregon Trail style covered wagon) up a hill with just a thick rope. The wagon is filled with all the people that we associate with. When you're pulling a wagon up a steep hill, you can't have any dead weight. It's the same in our lives. The people that are deadweight know our goals but don't help us. Whatever is at the top of that hill for you is what the people in the wagon need to assist with. If they aren't helping you move the wagon or clear the path then you need to boot them off the wagon.

Also, people learned the real me. I no longer had the drums, or my writing, or a joke, or an intelligent fact, or a social media profile to hide behind. The video shined a light on who I am and what I've dealt with at the core. It was unfiltered, unadulterated, no holds barred, stripped down and bare. A lot of people responded openly by how surprised and saddened they were, but the vast majority of the people I associate with scrolled right over the video or otherwise couldn't be bothered with my story. I want to remind you that Triplex Observation is observing people's actions, how they go about the action (their emotions and attitude), and (perhaps most importantly) what they don't do. The silence of the majority of the people I associate with spoke volumes about the weakness and fragility of what I considered my network.

Finally, the video opened up a lot of doors for me. Within the first week after the video was released I was interviewed for a prominent mental health podcast, contacted about appearing on two other podcasts, was asked to write a few guest blogs, and made a lot of great connections. Not only did the video scare away the people I wanted no part of, but it attracted the people with whom I wanted to associate.

Although this next thought belongs in another book that I'm planning, it bears mentioning here. I feel that society is a mirror and it reflects to us what we put out. If we're hard-working, mindful, and serious people then we will be put in places with other hard-working, mindful, and serious people. However if we're not genuine, guard ourselves, and go through life at half speed, then we'll be subjected to people of the similar ilk. With those two options, I feel the only logical choice is to be true to ourselves and pursue our passions and dreams with unbridled tenacity.

"And in the End"

I initially entitled this conclusion "Oh, that this too, too solid flesh would melt," to pay tribute to one of my favorite bands, Dream Theater. They used these lyrics to bring their song "Pull Me Under" to an abrupt, climactic conclusion. However, upon researching where the line originated (with respect to Mike Portnoy, the lyricist, I didn't believe he was capable of creating such a line- to my own credit, he didn't) I discovered it was from Shakespeare's Hamlet. It is from Hamlet's soliloquy in Act 1 Scene 2. In the irony of ironies, this quote from Hamlet is contained at the beginning of the character's lamenting his inability to commit suicide. The soliloquy continues, "Or that the everlasting had not fixed/ His cannon 'gainst self slaughter! Oh God! Oh God!" This was *not* how I wanted, nor will it be, the way I bring this book to a close.

The Beatles, "The End" is a great song and I believe the lyrics- with my interpretation- can help to sew everything together. The full lyric that I started in the title of this chapter is "And in the end/ The love you take/ Is equal to the love you make." If we interpret "love" as a tangible item or an emotion (rather than the action that Sir Paul McCartney alluded to) it makes sense that we must make or construct something before we can take or enjoy it. If we replace love with "success" then it ties the whole book together. "The success you take [enjoy] is equal to the success you make." Damn, I may frame that and put it in my office! OK, enough head shrinking hippie hymns.

My goals when I set out on this journey (aside from the professional freedom of leaving the prison) were quite simple. I wanted to share my story of abuse and living with undiagnosed mental health challenges to start to build a relationship and rapport with you. I wanted to share my personal journey thus far in seeking mental health care and improving my life. This was to humanize the whole experience, dispel demons surrounding the process of seeking mental health, and offer my assistance if you may need it. Lastly, I wanted to provide solid, tangible, immediate steps that we- everyone- can take to improve our lives and the lives of those around us.

I want to extend an invitation to connect. I want to build a community of cooperation and communication. The poet John Dunne wrote the poem "No Man Is an Island," and I have to agree with that. Reach out to me and allow me to help you to succeed. Buying this book was not a onetime transaction. I'm like a stray cat and you just fed me (please don't have me neutered). I wish to build a relationship with you. I didn't put my email in here a bazillion times for my health. Crush Complacency operates under the mantra of "Elevation through Education" and the best education I can provide as the resident certified life coach is one-on-one, case specific education, guidance, and coaching. I am on Facebook, Twitter, Instagram, Snapchat, LinkedIn, and YouTube. I am widely accessible through all of those media (in addition to my email) and I am the only one who responds under my name. I do not, and will never, have a ghost writer for my social media profiles or email. My connection to my audience is sacred and I refuse to allow anyone to mettle in that private relationship.

Education is a lifelong commitment and adventure. Jim Rohn said, "Formal education will make you a living. Self-education will make you a fortune." My goal is to develop a community of knowledgeable, self-educated people working in cooperation to elevate everyone around them and assist others to obtain their goals while we pursue ours. I believe that this model has the potential to enrich the whole world.

This isn't goodbye. This isn't even "See you soon." If you have gained but one little bit of useful information from these pages, and, most importantly, implement it into your life today, then I have reached my goal and we are inseparable. You have my idea and you can add it to your idea. However, the interaction is incomplete. What idea can you share with me?

I look forward to hearing from you soon, my friend.
Much love and respect,

"The Escape Artist"
AJ Nystrom

About the Author

"The Escape Artist" AJ Nystrom loves to help people and it is evident in his work. As a veteran of law enforcement of nine years, AJ entered the field to improve the quality of life for others and strengthen the fabric of his community. Unsatisfied with his impact as a federal agent with ICE and a correction officer with the Massachusetts Department of Correction he pursued becoming a certified life coach. Since obtaining his certification he has helped many in his community and beyond to create a clear design, take strategic steps, and make significant improvement to their lives.

In his personal time, AJ enjoys playing the drums, collecting vintage baseball cards, and renovating/modernizing his home that was built in 1860.

As an empath, humanitarian, and avid animal lover (though not a pet owner… yet) AJ enjoys volunteering with organizations that assist and empower people as well as serve the health, safety, and wellbeing of animals.

Made in the USA
Middletown, DE
02 July 2017